ATTACK OF THE
Deranged Mutant
Killer Monster
SNOW GOONS

Also by Bill Watterson:

CALVIN AND HOBBES
SOMETHING UNDER THE BED IS DROOLING
YUKON HO!
WEIRDOS FROM ANOTHER PLANET!
THE REVENGE OF THE BABY-SAT
THE CALVIN AND HOBBES LAZY SUNDAY BOOK
THE AUTHORITATIVE CALVIN AND HOBBES
SCIENTIFIC PROGRESS GOES 'BOINK'

ATTACK OF THE Deranged Mutant Killer Monster SNOW GOONS

A Calvin and Hobbes Collection by Bill Watterson

WARNER BOOKS

A *Warner* Book

First published in Great Britain in 1992
by Warner Books
First published in the USA by Andrews and McMeel 1992

ISBN 0 7474 1172 7

Printed and bound in Great Britain by
BPCC Hazells Ltd
Member of BPCC Ltd

Warner Books
A Division of
Little, Brown and Company (UK) Limited
165 Great Dover Street
London SE1 4YA

6

CALVIN and HOBBES

by WATTERSON

I'D SURE LIKE TO SHAKE THE HAND OF THE GENIUS WHO INVENTED THESE.

OK, HERE'S THE GAME: WE TOSS THE WATER BALLOON BACK AND FORTH, BUT EACH TIME WE CATCH IT, WE TAKE A STEP BACK. THE IDEA IS TO SEE HOW FAR APART WE CAN GET BEFORE ONE OF US GETS SOAKED.

GOTCHA.

OK, TOSS IT TO ME.

THERE, I CAUGHT IT! NOW WE TAKE A STEP BACK, AND I'LL TOSS IT TO YOU.

HA HA! CATCH THIS, SUCKER!

PLOOSH!

HA HA HA! WHAT A CHUMP! WHAT A NAÏF! HA HA HA!

HEY! WHAT'S THE MATTER? CAN'T YOU TAKE A JOKE?! IT WAS A JOKE! I MEAN, IT WAS AN ACCIDENT! I DIDN'T DO IT ON PURPOSE!

HEY! NO! NOT THE RAIN BARREL!

IT'S NO FUN TO PLAY GAMES WITH A POOR SPORT.

CAN I BE EXCUSED? THERE'S A TV SHOW I WANT TO SEE.

WE'RE STILL EATING DINNER, CALVIN.

I'M THROUGH. THIS STUFF WAS AWFUL. I WANT TO GO WATCH TELEVISION.

IT'S IMPOLITE TO LEAVE THE TABLE IN THE MIDDLE OF A MEAL.

SO WHAT AM I SUPPOSED TO DO? JUST *SIT* HERE AND WATCH YOU GUYS *CHEW*?! I'LL MISS MY SHOW!

YOUR TV SHOW ISN'T AS IMPORTANT AS SPENDING SOME TIME TOGETHER AS A FAMILY.

WE'LL COMPROMISE. I'LL GO WATCH A SITCOM FAMILY.

IN A MINUTE YOU'RE GOING TO DISCOVER THE DIFFERENCE BETWEEN THOSE AND REAL LIFE.

MY TV SHOW IS STARTING. I'M MISSING MY SHOW!

I'M SURE YOUR INSTINCT FOR SURVIVAL WILL KICK IN SHORTLY.

WHAT'S THE BIG DEAL ABOUT DINNER?! WHY CAN'T I GO WATCH TV? LOTS OF PEOPLE WATCH TV WHILE THEY EAT!

CALVIN, DINNER IS THE ONE TIME DURING THE DAY THAT WE SET ASIDE TO BE TOGETHER AND TALK. THERE'S MORE TO BEING A FAMILY THAN JUST LIVING IN THE SAME HOUSE. WE NEED TO INTERACT ONCE IN A WHILE.

WE COULD ALL ARGUE OVER WHAT CHANNEL TO WATCH.

YOU KNOW WHAT I MEAN.

I'VE MISSED HALF OF MY TV SHOW NOW. I HOPE YOU'RE HAPPY.

YOU SHOULDN'T BE PLANNING YOUR LIFE AROUND THE TV ANYWAY.

HMPH.

LOOK, I DON'T THINK IT'S TOO MUCH TO ASK THAT WE SIT TOGETHER FOR 40 MINUTES WITHOUT DISTRACTIONS AND INTERRUPTIONS.

RINNGG!

I'LL GET IT! I'M EXPECTING A CALL.

GO AHEAD, DAD. I BELIEVE YOU WERE SAYING SOMETHING FUNNY.

I HAVE ALL THESE GREAT GENES, BUT THEY'RE RECESSIVE. *THAT'S* THE PROBLEM HERE.

C'MON HOBBES, WE HAVE TO GO OUTSIDE.

WE *HAVE* TO?

YEAH, DAD WON'T LET ME WATCH TV. HE SAYS IT'S SUMMER, IT'S LIGHT LATE, AND I SHOULD GO RUN AROUND INSTEAD OF SITTING IN FRONT OF THE TUBE. CAN YOU BELIEVE IT?! WHAT A DICTATOR!

HOW CRUEL IT IS TO BE FORCED TO PLAY.

I'LL SHOW HIM. I REFUSE TO HAVE FUN.

OK, NEXT WE'LL RACE TO THAT TREE OVER THERE.

THIS RACE WILL DETERMINE THE CHAMPIONSHIP OF THE UNIVERSE.

OH... WAIT. HOW LONG HAVE WE BEEN OUT HERE?

I DUNNO. AN HOUR MAYBE.

REALLY? GEEZ, WHERE DOES THE TIME GO?! HANG ON, I'LL BE RIGHT BACK.

I'M *NOT* HAVING FUN!

IT'S GETTING DARK, CALVIN. TIME TO COME IN AND GO TO BED!

BUT HOBBES AND I WERE CATCHING FIREFLIES. CAN'T WE STAY OUT A LITTLE LONGER?

HA! FIRST YOU DIDN'T WANT TO GO OUT, AND NOW YOU DON'T WANT TO COME IN!

SEE, BY NOT WATCHING TV, YOU HAD MORE FUN, AND NOW YOU'LL HAVE MEMORIES OF SOMETHING REAL YOU *DID*, INSTEAD OF SOMETHING FAKE YOU JUST *WATCHED*.

NOTHING SPOILS FUN LIKE FINDING OUT IT BUILDS CHARACTER.

9

CALVIN and HOBBES

by WATTERSON

THE LATE CRETACEOUS...

..WHEN THE WORLD MEANT BUSINESS!

A GIGANTIC QUETZALCOATLUS, A PTEROSAUR THE SIZE OF AN AIRPLANE, SWOOPS OVER THE HORRIBLE TYRANNOSAURUS!

THE TYRANNOSAUR LUNGES AND BRINGS DOWN THE FLYING PEST!

UH OH! THE COMMOTION ATTRACTS *OTHER* TYRANNOSAURS, GREEDY FOR AN UNDESERVED PIECE!

PLEASE PASS ME A WING, CALVIN.

NO! YOU CAN'T HAVE ANY! IT'S MINE! ALL MINE!

DRIVEN AWAY BY THE FIERCE ROARING AND GNASHING OF THE INTRUDERS, THE TYRANNOSAUR NURSES A DEEP GRUDGE. REVENGE WILL SOON BE HIS!

HEY MOM, IF WE WERE CANNIBALS, WHAT PARTS OF PEOPLE WOULD WE EAT?

WHAT?! YOU KNOW, WHERE WOULD THE STEAKS BE? WOULD LEGS BE LIKE DRUMSTICKS? WOULD KIDS BE LIKE VEAL?

UGHH! GO BE DISGUSTING SOMEWHERE ELSE! OUT!

SOME PEOPLE JUST DON'T HAVE INQUISITIVE MINDS.

EVER NOTICE HOW THE OLDER PEOPLE GET, THE SLOWER THEY DO THINGS?

I WONDER WHY THAT IS. I WOULD THINK THAT THE LESS LIFE YOU HAD LEFT, THE FASTER YOU'D WANT TO DO EVERYTHING, SO YOU COULD PACK MORE INTO THE REMAINING YEARS.

YOU CAN BET WHEN I'M A GEEZER LIKE DAD, I'LL BE GOING LIKE A MANIAC.

OH GREAT.

BETTER HURRY. YOUR MOM'S YELLING SOMETHING.

CALVIN, WILL YOU TAKE THIS TO THE GARBAGE CAN IN THE GARAGE PLEASE?

THE *GARAGE*?? ARE YOU MAD?

I *WILL* BE, IF YOU DON'T HOP TO IT.

BUT THAT'S WHERE MY KILLER BICYCLE IS! I CAN'T GO OUT THERE! IT'LL JUMP ME!

I DON'T WANT ANY NONSENSE. JUST DO WHAT I ASKED, OK?

RRRRR

I WONDER HOW FAR FROM THIS HOUSE MY SAVINGS WOULD GET ME.

PSST! HOBBES!

WHAT ARE YOU DOING UP THERE?

HIDING FROM MY KILLER BICYCLE. IT CAN'T CLIMB TREES, SO I GUESS I'LL STAY HERE THE REST OF MY LIFE.

YOU SHOULD JUST WEDGE A BIG STICK THROUGH THE SPOKES OF THE FRONT WHEEL. THAT WAY WHEN THE STICK HITS THE FORK, THE WHEEL WILL JAM AND THE BIKE WILL FLIP OVER.

HEY, THAT'S *A GREAT* IDEA! HOBBES, YOU'RE A LIFESAVER!

WE COULD MOSEY OVER TO THE KITCHEN IF YOU'RE WONDERING HOW YOU CAN POSSIBLY THANK ME ENOUGH.

I DID IT, HOBBES! I DID JUST WHAT YOU SAID! I PUT A STICK IN THE SPOKES OF MY KILLER BICYCLE!

WHEN IT TRIED TO CHASE ME, IT FLIPPED OVER! I WRESTLED IT TO EXHAUSTION, AND THEN I LET THE AIR OUT OF ITS TIRES!

HA! I GUESS THAT NASTY OL' THING WON'T BE COMING AFTER *ME* ANY MORE! WE'RE TOO SMART FOR IT! MAN TRIUMPHS OVER MACHINE!

TRAINING WHEELS! WHAT A GOOD IDEA!

I PUMPED UP HIS TIRES TOO. THEY WERE BOTH FLAT.

A TOAST TO US! TO US!

BEST FRIENDS FOREVER! RIGHT!

CRUNCH CRUNCH CRUNCH CRUNCH

HI DAD. I SUPPOSE YOU'RE WONDERING HOW YOU'RE DOING IN THE POLLS. NOT REALLY.

I THINK YOU'LL FIND *THIS* CHART QUITE REVEALING. THIS LINE REPRESENTS THE "AVERAGE DAD APPROVAL RATING" OF 70%. THIS OVERLAY SHOWS *YOUR* APPROVAL RATING AT JUST UNDER *10%*!

HOUSEHOLD SIX-YEAR-OLDS WERE POLLED ON THEIR FAVORITE BEDTIMES. WATCH ON THESE SUCCESSIVE OVERLAYS HOW YOUR RATING WOULD IMPROVE WITH EACH HOUR LATER! SEE, BY MIDNIGHT, YOU'RE RIGHT UP TO NORMAL!

THESE FINDINGS SUGGEST A LOGICAL COURSE OF ACTION. HOW LONG DO YOU SPEND MAKING THESE CHARTS?

MY TIGER, IT SEEMS, IS RUNNING 'ROUND NUDE.
THIS FUR COAT MUST HAVE MADE HIM PERSPIRE.
IT LIES ON THE FLOOR—SHOULD THIS BE CONSTRUED
AS A PERMANENT CHANGE OF ATTIRE?
PERHAPS HE CONSIDERS ITS COLORS PASSÉ,
OR MAYBE IT FIT HIM TOO SNUG
WILL HE WANT IT BACK? SHOULD I PUT IT AWAY?
OR USE IT RIGHT HERE AS A RUG?

I WONDER WHEN SCHOOL STARTS.

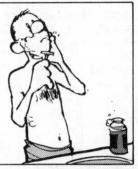

Calvin and Hobbes

by WATTERSON

ANOTHER DAY, ANOTHER DOLLAR...

... ANOTHER IRREPLACEABLE CHUNK OUT OF A FINITE AND RAPIDLY PASSING LIFETIME.

WHAT A BEAUTIFUL SUMMER DAY... AND I'VE GOT TO SPEND IT IN AN OFFICE. BROTHER.

IT SEEMS LIKE I'M ALWAYS RUSHING OFF AND NEVER TAKING THE TIME TO ENJOY DAYS LIKE THIS.

I'D SURE LIKE TO HAVE A QUIET DAY AROUND THE HOUSE. NO TRAFFIC, NO SCHEDULE, NO PHONE CALLS... BOY, THAT WOULD BE GREAT. I COULD SPEND SOME TIME WITH CALVIN, READ A BOOK, GO ON A BIKE RIDE...

MAYBE I SHOULD TAKE THE DAY OFF. THE WORLD WOULDN'T END IF I DIDN'T GO INTO THE OFFICE TODAY. DAYS LIKE THIS DON'T COME OFTEN AND LIFE IS SHORT.

WATTERSON

HI DAD. BYE DAD.

NUGHH

YOU GET BACK HERE AND PICK EVERY ONE OF THOSE DEAD BUGS OUT OF MY SHAMPOO!! I MEAN *NOW!*

WITH A DISTANT RUMBLING, GREAT THUNDER CLOUDS PILE HIGH INTO THE SKY!

SUDDENLY THERE'S A BLINDING FLASH OF LIGHT! IT'S CALVIN THE LIGHTNING BOLT!

IN A FRACTION OF A SECOND, THE HOUSE BELOW WILL BE IN A MILLION PIECES!

I KNOW IT'S RAINING OUT, BUT PLAY A BOARD GAME OR SOMETHING.

EVERY DAY IT'S THE SAME OLD THING.

... BUT NOT TODAY!

EVERYBODY'S A SLAVE TO ROUTINE.

CAN I GET SOME CONTACT LENSES?

YOUR EYES ARE FINE! YOU DON'T NEED CONTACTS.

YES I DO! THEY HAVE SOME THAT CHANGE THE COLOR OF YOUR EYES!

YOUR EYES ARE VERY PRETTY THE WAY THEY ARE.

BUT IF I HAD CONTACTS, I COULD MAKE ONE EYE BLOOD RED AND THE OTHER YELLOW STRIPED, LIKE A BUG.

I DUNNO, IT SEEMS LIKE ONCE PEOPLE GROW UP, THEY HAVE NO IDEA WHAT'S COOL.

GEEZ, I GOTTA HAVE A *REASON* FOR EVERYTHING?!

BOY, WHEN IT'S *THIS* HOT, I DON'T WANT TO DO ANYTHING AT ALL!

FORTUNATELY, THAT WAS OUR PLAN FROM THE START.

ME, TARZAN! KING OF JUNGLE!

THUMP THUMP

NICE UNDERPANTS. DOES YOUR MOM KNOW YOU'RE OVER HERE LIKE THIS?

I DON'T THINK JANE *EVER* SAID THAT TO TARZAN.

CalviN and HoBbEs
by WATTERSON

TO MAKE INSTANT FUN...

... JUST ADD WATER!

HEH HEH HEH FWOOSH!

HEE HEE

LOOKING FOR SOMEONE?

UH, WHO? *ME??* HA HA HA HA HA! UM, NO-O, I MEAN, YES...BUT SOMEONE *ELSE.* HEH HEH. NOT YOU.

HERE'S A HYPOTHETICAL QUESTION YOU SHOULD ASK YOURSELF.

IF YOU KNEW TODAY WAS YOUR LAST DAY ON EARTH, WHAT WOULD YOU DO DIFFERENT?

...*ESPECIALLY* IF, BY DOING SOMETHING *DIFFERENT,* TODAY MIGHT *NOT* BE YOUR LAST DAY ON EARTH.

I DON'T THINK THAT QUESTION WAS VERY HYPOTHETICAL AT ALL.

OH BOY! COOKED-OUT HAMBURGERS!

THEY MAY BE CHARRED ON THE OUTSIDE! THEY MAY BE RAW ON THE INSIDE! BUT AT LEAST THEY'VE GOT THAT SPECIAL OUTDOOR FLAVOR!

... OF LIGHTER FLUID! MM-MM, WHEN DO WE EAT?

WHADDAYA *MEAN* TOMORROW?!

I LIKE TOYS THAT MAKE A LOT OF RACKET.

THAT'S THE PROBLEM WITH THIS WAGON. IT DOESN'T MAKE MUCH NOISE.

NIEEEE!! AUGH! WHOAA!

OOMPH! OOH!

FORTUNATELY, *WE* DO.

YAAH!

OOPS.

HE JUST DOES THAT TO SHOW HE *COULD'VE* SNUFFED ME.

HELLO?

HI DAD! IT'S ME, CALVIN.

CALVIN, UNLESS THIS IS *REALLY* IMPORTANT, HANG UP, OK? I'M VERY BUSY.

OK, DAD. GOODBYE.

THIS SHOULD QUALIFY IN ANOTHER 15 MINUTES.

CALVIN, I ASKED YOU TO CLEAN UP YOUR ROOM.

I *DID!*

WELL, YOU DIDN'T DO A VERY GOOD JOB THEN. IT LOOKS AS MESSY AS IT DID BEFORE.

YOU SHOULD TAKE PRIDE IN WHAT YOU DO, AND ALWAYS DO THE BEST JOB POSSIBLE.

I DON'T NEED TO DO A BETTER JOB. I NEED BETTER P.R. ON THE JOB I *DO.*

HUHH

UHH!

I WOULDN'T BE WORRIED ABOUT THIS IF HE WAS A BETTER STUDENT.

26

CALVIN and HOBBES

by WATTERSON

SHEESH. YOU BUY THE KID A GOOD, EXPENSIVE LOCK, AND LOOK.

THIS MEETING OF TOP-SECRET CLUB G.R.O.S.S. (GET RID OF SLIMY GIRLS) WILL COME TO ORDER, SUPREME RULER AND DICTATOR-FOR-LIFE CALVIN PRESIDING!

HEAR HEAR!

PRESIDENT AND FIRST TIGER HOBBES WILL NOW PROVIDE US WITH AN ATTENDANCE REPORT.

ALL PRESENT AND ACCOUNTED FOR, SIR!

EXCELLENT! NOW CLUB SECRETARY GENERAL HOBBES WILL REVIEW THE MINUTES.

IT'S 10:32.

THANK YOU. AT THIS TIME WE'LL HAVE A FIELD REPORT FROM TOP SCOUT CALVIN!

YOU CAN TELL THIS IS A GREAT CLUB BECAUSE WE HAVE SO MANY OFFICERS.

HEREWITH, A FIELD REPORT FROM HEAD SCOUT CALVIN!

WHAT NEWS, SCOUT?

THE ENEMY HAS BEEN SIGHTED ON THE SIDEWALK TWO DOORS DOWN, MR. PRESIDENT.

THE ENEMY?

SUSIE DERKINS, AN ACKNOWLEDGED GIRL! I RECOMMEND WE ESTABLISH A STRIKE FORCE!

ITS OBJECTIVE?

TO BUG HER!

SOUNDS RISKY, MEN. ANY VOLUNTEERS?

OK, HERE'S OUR PLAN. I'LL BE THE STRIKE FORCE COMMANDER. YOU'LL BE THE SPECIAL AGENT IN CHARGE OF MUNITIONS.

WE'LL FILL UP A WATER BALLOON AND SNEAK UP ON SUSIE THROUGH THE BACK YARD!

I GET TO BE THE OFFICIAL CARTOGRAPHER AND MAP OUR HIDING PLACES AND ESCAPE ROUTES!

YEAH! AND I'LL BE THE CODE EXPERT AND MAKE AN UNBREAKABLE CODE!

OH BOY! LET'S GET SOME PAPER!

I HOPE SUSIE DOESN'T GO ANYPLACE FOR A WHILE.

OK, HERE'S THE UNITED STATES...

THERE! I FINISHED OUR SECRET CODE!

LET'S SEE.

I ASSIGNED EACH LETTER A TOTALLY RANDOM NUMBER, SO THE CODE WILL BE HARD TO CRACK. FOR LETTER "A," YOU WRITE 3,004,572,688. "B" IS 28,731,569½.

THAT'S A GOOD CODE ALL RIGHT.

NOW WE JUST COMMIT THIS TO MEMORY.

DID YOU FINISH YOUR MAP OF OUR NEIGHBORHOOD?

NOT YET. HOW MANY BRICKS DOES THE FRONT WALK HAVE?

WE'VE GOT OUR MAP, OUR CODE, AND OUR WATER BALLOON! LET'S GO SOAK SUSIE!

OUR MAP SAYS FIRST WE RUN TO THE BIG TREE OUT BACK.

NOW TO THE BUSH OUT FRONT!

NOW TO THE DITCH OUT BACK!

NOW TO THE TREE OUT FRONT!

IN CASE YOU'RE WONDERING ...THIS IS TO LOSE ANYONE WHO MIGHT BE TAILING US.

I'M WRITING YOU A MESSAGE IN CODE. HOW DO YOU SPELL "NINCOMPOOP"?

WE MADE IT TO SUSIE'S YARD!

BUT WHERE'S SUSIE? I DON'T SEE HER!

ARGHH! WE GO TO ALL THIS TROUBLE TO LAUNCH AN ATTACK ON HER, AND WHAT DOES SHE DO? SHE *MOVES*! ALL OUR GREAT PLANS ARE FOR NAUGHT! A WHOLE MORNING RUINED!

MAYBE SHE JUST WENT IN FOR LUNCH. SEE, SHE LEFT SOME OF HER TOYS OUT, SO SHE'S PROBABLY PLANNING TO COME BACK.

THAT GIVES ME A *FABULOUS* IDEA!

UH OH.

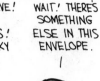

IT'S A *RANSOM* NOTE! THAT DIRTY CALVIN STOLE MY DOLL AND HE WANTS ME TO PAY $100 TO GET HER BACK!

OF ALL THE NERVE! HE CAN'T GET AWAY WITH THIS! WHY, THAT STINKY LITTLE...

WAIT! THERE'S SOMETHING ELSE IN THIS ENVELOPE.

A PHOTO OF BINKY BETSY TIED TO A CHAIR!!

WHAT A GREAT CLUB!

HOW ARE YOU GOING TO SPEND *YOUR* $50?

LET'S STROLL DOWN THE SIDEWALK *REAL CASUALLY* AND SEE IF SUSIE PUT THE HUNDRED BUCKS OUT BY THE TREE YET.

GREAT!

LOVELY DAY FOR A STROLL, EH HOBBES? I CERTAINLY ENJOY MY AFTERNOON CONSTITUTIONAL!

YES, IT'S QUITE INVIGORATING!

LOOK! LOOK! THERE'S THE ENVELOPE! SHE DID IT! WE'RE RICH!

OH BOY! LET'S SNEAK UP AND GET IT!

C'MON, YOU LOUSE. C'MONNN...

I DON'T SEE SUSIE. DO YOU?

YOU STAND GUARD AND WATCH FOR SUSIE WHILE I COUNT THE MONEY AND MAKE SURE IT'S ALL THERE!

HEY, THERE'S NO MONEY IN HERE AT ALL! THERE'S JUST A NOTE!

IT SAYS, "NOW WE'RE EVEN!" NOW WE'RE EVEN?? WHAT'S *THAT* SUPPOSED TO MEAN?!

HOBBES? HOBBES!

COME BACK HERE WITH HOBBES! PUT HIM DOWN! HOBBES, BITE HER! BITE HER!

HA HA! NYAHH! NYAHH!

SLAM

GET AWAY FROM OUR DOOR WITH THAT DRILL!

OOOH, THAT ROTTEN SUSIE! I HATE HER! I HATE HER! SHE'D BETTER SET HOBBES FREE!

SO I KIDNAPPED HER STUPID DOLL! SHE DIDN'T NEED TO *RETALIATE!* CAN'T SHE TAKE A *JOKE?!*

GIRLS HAVE **NO** SENSE OF HUMOR! THAT'S THEIR WHOLE PROBLEM!

ALL THIS WAS FUNNY UNTIL SHE DID THE SAME THING TO ME.

ALL RIGHT, SUSIE, I BROUGHT YOUR DUMB DOLL BACK! NOW LET HOBBES OUT, OK? FAIR'S FAIR!

I DUNNO, CALVIN. I'M THINKING I MIGHT RATHER HAVE YOUR TIGER. YOU CAN KEEP BINKY BETSY.

AAHH! I DON'T WANT A *DOLL!* THIS IS YOURS! TAKE IT!

OH, YOU'LL GROW TO LIKE HER, CALVIN. SHE HAS THE CUTEST ACCESSORIES YOU CAN BUY!

NO! NO! I WANT HOBBES! TAKE THIS!

BUT I THINK HOBBES LIKES IT BETTER HERE WITH **ME.**

HE DOES NOT!

LOOK SUSIE, I'LL GIVE YOU YOUR DOLL **AND** I'LL GIVE YOU A QUARTER, OK? IT'S ALL I HAVE. WILL YOU LET HOBBES OUT **NOW** ??

ALL RIGHT, HERE. AND NEXT TIME, LEAVE MY STUFF ALONE. GOT IT?

RIGHT! SURE!

JERK.

WHAT KIND OF TIGER **ARE** YOU ?! YOU DIDN'T EVEN MAUL HER! WHAT WERE YOU **DOING** THERE ?!

WOULDN'T **YOU** LIKE TO KNOW!

I'VE GOT TO SAY, HOBBES, IT DOESN'T GIVE OUR CLUB A LOT OF CREDIT WHEN THE FIRST TIGER IS A WILLING CAPTIVE OF THE ENEMY.

THBPTB

WE STOLE **HER** DOLL, AND **I'M** THE ONE WHO HAD TO PAY RANSOM! IT'S A DISGRACE!

YOU GET 15 DEMERITS FOR BESMIRCHING THE CLUB'S REPUTATION, PLUS FIVE DEMERITS FOR CONDUCT UNBECOMING AN OFFICER, AND A CENSURE IN THE CLUB BOOK FOR NOT DEVOURING SUSIE WHEN YOU HAD THE CHANCE. HMM, ANYTHING ELSE?

I ALMOST TOLD HER OUR CODE WHEN SHE RUBBED MY TUMMY.

GOOD GRAVY, WHOSE SIDE ARE YOU ON ?!

WELL, THIS IS CERTAINLY A SORRY CHAPTER IN G.R.O.S.S. HISTORY! FIRST TIGER HOBBES, A TRAITOR TO THE CAUSE!

IT MIGHT INTEREST YOU TO KNOW THAT AFTER I WON SUSIE'S CONFIDENCE, I DID SOME SPYING.

SPYING? YOU WERE A SPY ??

I READ AN OPEN PAGE OF SUSIE'S DIARY.

WOW! DEEP IN ENEMY TERRITORY, YOU INTERCEPTED A SECRET MESSAGE? WHAT DID IT SAY ??

IT SAID, "CALVIN IS A PIG-FACED SMELLY FAT-HEAD!"

THEN OUR CLUB IS A SUCCESS! BRILLIANT WORK, HOBBES! PROMOTIONS FOR EVERYONE! WELCOME BACK!

HELP ME WITH THIS HOMEWORK, OK? WHAT'S 6+3?

6+3, EH? WELL, THIS ONE IS A BIT TRICKY.

FIRST WE CALL THE ANSWER "Y," AS IN "Y DO WE CARE?" NOW Y MAY BE A SQUARE NUMBER, SO WE'LL DRAW A SQUARE AND MAKE THIS SIDE 6 AND THAT SIDE 3. THEN WE'LL MEASURE THE DIAGONAL.

I DON'T REMEMBER THE TEACHER EXPLAINING IT LIKE THIS.

SHE PROBABLY DOESN'T KNOW HIGHER MATH. WHEN YOU DEAL WITH HIGH NUMBERS, YOU NEED HIGHER MATH.

BUT THIS DIAGONAL IS JUST A LITTLE UNDER TWO.

OK, HERE, I'LL DRAW A BIGGER SQUARE.

HEY, NO COMIC BOOKS UNTIL YOU FINISH YOUR HOMEWORK.

I DID FINISH.

THAT DIDN'T TAKE VERY LONG. DID YOU DO A GOOD JOB?

I DID A GREAT JOB. WHEN YOU'RE AS FAR AHEAD OF THE CLASS AS I AM, IT DOESN'T TAKE MUCH TIME.

WELL WE'LL SEE ABOUT THAT WHEN I GET BACK FROM MY PARENT-TEACHER CONFERENCE WITH MISS WORMWOOD.

YOU'RE GOING TO TALK TO MY TEACHER?

I'M SURE IT WILL BE AN INFORMATIVE MEETING.

GOSH, I FORGOT TO TELL YOU! MISS WORMWOOD SAID I WAS SO GOOD, YOU DIDN'T NEED TO BOTHER COMING! REALLY! SHE SAID YOU DON'T HAVE TO GO!

OH MAN! MOM WENT TO A PARENT-TEACHER CONFERENCE! I'M AS GOOD AS DEAD! MISS WORMWOOD WILL TELL MOM ALL SORTS OF HORROR STORIES ABOUT ME!

HORROR STORIES?

WELL, IT'S ALL A QUESTION OF PERSPECTIVE. STILL, I THINK I SHOULD BE ALLOWED TO HAVE A LAWYER PRESENT AT THE MEETING.

WHAT ARE YOU GOING TO SAY WHEN YOUR MOM GETS BACK?

NOTHING.

NOTHING AT ALL?

BUDDY, IF YOU THINK I'M EVEN GOING TO BE HERE, YOU'RE CRAZY!

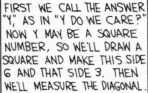

Panel 1: I'M HOME.

HOW WAS YOUR MEETING WITH CALVIN'S TEACHER?

Panel 2: WELL, WHEN WE GOT TO THE CLASSROOM, WE SAW THAT ALL THE KIDS HAD DRAWN SELF-PORTRAITS IN ART CLASS, AND HAD LEFT THE PICTURES ON THEIR DESKS SO THE PARENTS WOULD RECOGNIZE THEIR CHILD'S SEAT.

Panel 3: THAT'S A CUTE IDEA. DID YOU FIND CALVIN'S PICTURE?

THERE WAS ONE DRAWING OF A GREEN KID WITH FANGS, SIX EYES, AND HIS FINGER UP HIS NOSE.

Panel 4: UH OH.

THE MEETING WENT DOWNHILL FROM THERE.

Panel 5: CALVIN, I...

YIKE!! YOU'RE HOME! I DIDN'T EVEN FINISH PACK... ..THAT IS, UM...

Panel 6: LIES! EVERYTHING MISS WORMWOOD SAID ABOUT ME WAS A LIE! SHE JUST DOESN'T LIKE ME! SHE HATES LITTLE BOYS! IT'S NOT MY FAULT! I'M NOT TO BLAME!

Panel 7: SHE TOLD YOU ABOUT THE NOODLES, RIGHT? IT WASN'T ME! NOBODY SAW ME! I WAS FRAMED! I WOULDN'T DO ANYTHING LIKE THAT! I'M INNOCENT, I TELL YOU!

Panel 8: WHAT NOODLES?

OH .... UH .... HA HA! DID I SAY NOODLES? YOU MUST HAVE HEARD WRONG. I DIDN'T SAY NOODLES.

Panel 9: OK CALVIN, LET'S CHECK OVER YOUR MATH HOMEWORK.

LET'S NOT, AND SAY WE DID.

Panel 10: YOUR TEACHER SAYS YOU NEED TO SPEND MORE TIME ON IT. HAVE A SEAT.

MORE TIME?! I ALREADY SPENT TEN WHOLE MINUTES ON IT! TEN MINUTES SHOT! WASTED! DOWN THE DRAIN!

Panel 11: YOU'VE WRITTEN HERE 8+4=7. NOW YOU KNOW THAT'S NOT RIGHT.

SO I WAS OFF A LITTLE BIT. SUE ME.

Panel 12: YOU CAN'T ADD THINGS AND COME OUT WITH LESS THAN YOU STARTED WITH!

I CAN DO THAT! IT'S A FREE COUNTRY! I'VE GOT MY RIGHTS!

LET'S START AT THE BEGINNING. WHEN YOU **ADD** SOMETHING, YOU **INCREASE** WHAT YOU HAVE. YOU **COMBINE**.

I DON'T WANT TO LEARN THIS! IT'S COMPLETELY IRRELEVANT TO MY LIFE!

THIS ISN'T IRRELEVANT. EVERYONE NEEDS TO KNOW THIS.

I DON'T! I CAN GET ALONG FINE WITHOUT MATH!

OH YEAH? WHAT DO YOU WANT TO BE WHEN YOU GROW UP? EVERY JOB REQUIRES **SOME** MATH.

THAT'S NOT TRUE! I'LL BE A... A...

.."A CAVEMAN! YEAH!

THAT'S NOT REALLY A JOB.

HERE, MAYBE THIS WILL MAKE MORE SENSE. I HAVE EIGHT PENNIES. I ASK YOU FOR FOUR MORE.

I SAY FORGET IT. YOU'RE THE ONE WITH A STEADY PAYCHECK.

JUST GIVE ME FOUR PENNIES. GOOD. HOW MUCH MONEY DO I HAVE NOW?

INVESTMENTS AND ALL?

NO, JUST HERE ON THE TABLE.

EIGHT CENTS.

NO, EIGHT PLUS FOUR IS TWELVE. SEE? COUNT THEM UP.

BUT THOSE FOUR ARE **MINE**!

HOW'S THE MATH LESSON GOING?

PRETTY GOOD. I THINK CALVIN SEES THE IDEA NOW.

I TOOK PENNIES AND SHOWED HOW ADDING AND SUBTRACTING THEM CHANGED HOW MUCH MONEY HE HAD. IT'S NOT SO ABSTRACT THAT WAY.

GOOD. MAYBE HE'LL DO BETTER IN CLASS NOW.

I THINK HE WILL. HE WAS HAVING FUN WITH IT BY THE END.

NOW GIVE ME **ANOTHER** FIVE CENTS AND LET'S SEE WHAT I HAVE!

WAIT A MINUTE.

37

Panel 1: BOY, I FEEL SHARP! I KNOW THIS MATH STUFF *COLD!* I'M READY FOR ANYTHING!

Panel 2: I HOPE THE TEACHER CALLS ON ME! I HOPE I GET TO DEMONSTRATE A PROBLEM AT THE BOARD! I'LL IMPRESS EVERYONE!

Panel 3: HERE, SUSIE. TAKE ONE SHEET AND PASS THE REST ACROSS.

WHAT'S THIS?

Panel 4: A MATH QUIZ.

HOT DOG!

Panel 5: DON'T TRY TO COPY MY ANSWERS THIS TIME, CALVIN, OR I'LL TELL.

HA! WHO NEEDS *YOUR* ANSWERS?! I'LL BET I GET A BETTER SCORE THAN YOU DO.

Panel 6: *YOU?!* THAT'LL BE THE DAY!

I'LL BET YOU 25 CENTS I GET A HIGHER GRADE.

Panel 7: YOU'RE ON.

YOU MIGHT AS WELL GIVE ME THE QUARTER NOW AND SAVE YOURSELF THE HUMILIATION LATER!

Panel 8: MAYBE YOU'D LIKE TO INCREASE THE WAGER, MR. BIGMOUTH.

YEAH! LET'S DOUBLE IT AND MAKE IT *35* CENTS!

Panel 9: MAN, THIS IS GOING TO BE GREAT! NOT ONLY AM I GOING TO ACE THIS QUIZ, BUT I'M GOING TO WIN A QUARTER FROM SUSIE WHEN I GET A BETTER SCORE THAN SHE DOES!

Panel 10: OK! THE FIRST PROBLEM IS 6+5. OH, EASY! THE ANSWER IS... UM...

Panel 11: ..UMMMMMMMM...

Panel 12: UMMMM MMMM

HIS SPACECRAFT QUIETLY HUMMING, THE INCREDIBLE *SPACEMAN SPIFF* APPROACHES THE SIXTH PLANET OF THE MYSTERIO SYSTEM!

Panel 1: HOW CAN OUR TIME BE UP?! I JUST DID THE FIRST PROBLEM ON THIS QUIZ! WHERE DID THE TIME GO??

Panel 2: GUESS! GUESS! PICK RANDOM NUMBERS! MAYBE A FEW WILL BE RIGHT BY SHEER LUCK! 15! 104! 3! 27!

Panel 3: HAND IT IN, CALVIN. YOUR TIME'S UP. SIGHHHH

Panel 4: DON'T FORGET WE HAVE A BET ON WHO GETS THE HIGHER GRADE. THE BET'S OFF! I DON'T GAMBLE! NO BETS!

Panel 5: I GOT A PERFECT SCORE ON MY QUIZ. YOU GOT A PERFECT SCORE??

Panel 6: WHAT DID YOU GET? IF YOU MISSED ANY, YOU OWE ME 25 CENTS. I RAN OUT OF TIME! I'D HAVE HAD A PERFECT SCORE TOO IF I'D HAD A FEW MORE MINUTES!

Panel 7: WHAT DID YOU GET? IT'S **BIOLOGICAL**! GIRLS MATURE FASTER THAN BOYS! YOU JUST GOT A BETTER GRADE BECAUSE YOU'RE A GIRL! IT'S NOT FAIR!

Panel 8: PAY UP. MAYBE IT'S OPPOSITE DAY! MAYBE ALL THESE X's MEAN MY ANSWERS ARE **CORRECT**! MAYBE YOUR "A" IS REALLY AN "F"! THAT MUST BE IT! I WIN THE BET!

Panel 9: HOW DID YOU DO ON YOUR MATH QUIZ? I FLUNKED IT ...BUT ONLY BECAUSE I RAN OUT OF TIME.

Panel 10: THE WORST PART, THOUGH, WAS THAT SUSIE DERKINS WON OUR BET ON WHO'D GET THE BETTER SCORE. I HAD TO PAY HER 25 CENTS.

Panel 11: BUT GET THIS! I CHEATED HER! I ONLY GAVE HER THREE DIMES! HA!

Panel 12: I THINK YOU'D BETTER STUDY HARDER. OH, NOW DON'T *YOU* START ON ME.

CALVIN and HOBBES
by WATTERSON

BUTTONS.... CHECK.
DIALS .... CHECK.
SWITCHES ... CHECK.
LITTLE COLORED
LIGHTS ...... CHECK.

CALVIN, THE AIRLINE PILOT, IS TENTH IN LINE FOR TAKEOFF. HIS PATIENCE IS AT AN END!

IGNORING THE CONTROL TOWER'S PROTESTS, CALVIN GUNS THE ENGINES AND PASSES THE OTHER PLANES, CUTTING ACROSS LESS CROWDED RUNWAYS!

ROUNDING A CORNER, HE OPENS THE THROTTLE! STEWARDESSES EXPLAINING THE AIRCRAFT'S SAFETY FEATURES ARE HURLED TO THE REAR OF THE PLANE BY THE SUDDEN ACCELERATION!

ALL THE OTHER PLANES WATCH WITH ENVY AS CALVIN TAKES OFF AHEAD OF SCHEDULE!

BUT WHAT'S THIS?! ANOTHER PLANE HAD ALREADY RECEIVED CLEARANCE TO LAND! IT'S HEADED FOR THE SAME RUNWAY!

IT LOOKS LIKE A MID-AIR COLLISION OVER A CROWDED SUPER HIGHWAY AT RUSH HOUR! OH, WHAT A PRICE TO PAY FOR HIS HURRY!

I'M BACK! THANKS FOR WAITING SO PATIENTLY.

I COULD WAIT EVEN LONGER IF YOU'D BUY ME A THIRD PLANE.

CALVIN and HOBBES

by WATTERSON

UH OH. HERE COMES SUSIE.

TRY NOT TO BREATHE IN.

HERE, CALVIN.

WHAT'S THIS?

IT'S AN INVITATION. MR. BUN IS HOSTING A MILK AND COOKIE PARTY IN TEN MINUTES, AND YOU AND HOBBES ARE INVITED.

WE DECLINE!

WE WOULDN'T ATTEND IF YOU *PAID* US! WE'VE GOT BETTER THINGS TO DO THAN SIT AROUND WITH *GIRLS* AND DUMB TOY ANIMALS!

FINE! *DON'T* COME! WHO CARES?!

WHAT A JERK. ...I WENT TO ALL THIS TROUBLE, TOO.

DON'T BE DISAPPOINTED, MR. BUN. WE CAN HAVE A NICE PARTY ALL BY OURSELVES.

PHOOEY.

HA! WE SHOWED *HER*! ALL GIRLS SHOULD BE SHIPPED TO PLUTO — THAT'S WHAT *I* SAY.

I WONDER WHAT KIND OF COOKIES THEY WERE.

YOU CAME!

WE DON'T *ATTEND* PARTIES. WE JUST *CRASH* 'EM!

LOOK, HOBBES, I CUT A PIECE OF CARDBOARD TO MAKE A TV SCREEN.

SEE, I JUST HOLD IT UP AND IT'S LIKE I'M ON TV.

WOW, YOUR OWN SHOW!

TOO BAD I CAN'T REALLY FORCE MY WAY INTO MILLIONS OF PEOPLE'S HOMES EACH DAY.

BUT ON THE OTHER HAND, NO ONE IN *THIS* HOME CAN TURN ME OFF!

SO WHAT'S IT LIKE BEING ON TV?

IT'S GREAT!

NOW THAT I'M ON TELEVISION, I'M DIFFERENT FROM EVERYBODY ELSE! I'M FAMOUS! IMPORTANT!

SINCE EVERYONE KNOWS ME, EVERYTHING I DO NOW IS NEWSWORTHY. I'M A CULTURAL ICON.

I THINK YOUR ANTENNA NEEDS ADJUSTING.

WATCH, I'LL USE MY PRESTIGE TO ENDORSE A PRODUCT!

HI, I'M CALVIN, EMINENT TELEVISION PERSONALITY, HERE TO TELL YOU ABOUT NEW, IMPROVED "CHOCOLATE FROSTED SUGAR BOMBS"! I LOVE 'EM!

THEY'RE CRUNCHY ON THE OUTSIDE, CHEWY ON THE INSIDE, AND THEY DON'T HAVE A SINGLE NATURAL INGREDIENT OR ESSENTIAL VITAMIN TO GET IN THE WAY OF THAT RICH, FUDGY TASTE! MM-MM!

YES KIDS, YOU'LL LIKE 'EM SO MUCH, YOU WON'T BE ABLE TO SIT STILL! REMEMBER! IT'S THE CEREAL I GET PAID TO RECOMMEND BECAUSE I'M FAMOUS!

WHAT DO YOU THINK? ARE YOU FILLED WITH THE DESIRE TO EMULATE ME AND EAT THE CEREAL I ENDORSE? IF NOT, I CAN REPEAT THIS EVERY 20 MINUTES.

DON'T YOU THREATEN *ME*.

HI MOM! I'VE GOT MY OWN TV SHOW!

THAT'S NICE.

♪ HE'S CA·A·ALVIN! AMAZING, GREAT CA·A·ALVIN! OH, HE'S THE ONE THAT YOU'D LIKE TO MEET! HE'S THE ONE WHO JUST CAN'T BE BEAT! HE'S CA·A·ALVIN! LA DA TA DA DAAAAA! ♪

THANK YOU! THANK YOU! BOY, WHAT AN AUDIENCE! THANK YOU! PLEASE! HA HA! NO, REALLY, SIT DOWN! THANK YOU! THANK YOU!

I'M CHANGING THE CHANNEL, OK?

SORRY, I'M ON ALL THE NETWORKS.

WHERE'S YOUR TV SCREEN?

MY FALL LINEUP GOT CANCELED.

DAD SAID ONE TV IN THE HOUSE WAS BAD ENOUGH, AND HE PREFERRED THE ONE WITH THE VOLUME CONTROL.

MAYBE YOU SHOULD GO CABLE.

I'VE GOT AN IDEA FOR A SIT-COM CALLED "FATHER KNOWS ZILCH."

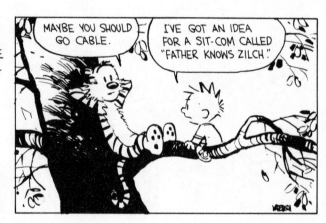

WHAT A RIP-OFF! THEY SAY IF YOU CONNECT THESE DOTS YOU GET A PICTURE, BUT LOOK! I DID IT AND IT'S JUST A BIG MESS!

I THINK YOU'RE SUPPOSED TO CONNECT THEM IN THE ORDER THAT THEY'RE NUMBERED.

OH.

EVERYTHING'S GOTTA HAVE RULES, RULES, RULES!

CALVIN and HOBBES

by WATTERSON

WELL! PEANUT BUTTER!

"...OR SO IT *SEEMS*.

DID YOU SEE THAT?

HMM? WHAT?

MY SANDWICH WIGGLED! THERE'S SOMETHING *ALIVE* IN IT!

OH STOP IT, CALVIN.

I'M NOT KIDDING! MOM MUST BE TRYING TO KILL ME! I BET THERE'S A SLUG IN MY PEANUT BUTTER!

EWW!

HMM... I DON'T *FEEL* ANY SLUGS IN HERE. WHAT COULD IT BE? I'D BETTER SMELL IT.

AUGH! AUGH! IT'S GOT MY NOSE!! THE PEANUT BUTTER *ITSELF* IS ALIVE!

IT'S OOZING UP MY FACE! IT'S GOING TO SUCK OUT MY EYEBALLS! HELP!

RRGH! MMF! BLRGHGH!

I GOT IT OFF! QUICK! DROWN IT IN CHOCOLATE MILK!

BOY, WHAT A CLOSE CALL *THAT* WAS! WON'T MOM BE DISAPPOINTED TO SEE HER LITTLE PLOT *FAILED!*

LOOK AT YOU! I'VE NEVER *SEEN* ANYTHING SO REVOLTING! WHAT'S WRONG WITH YOU?!

I'M EATING SOMEWHERE ELSE.

GIRLS ARE SO WEIRD.

45

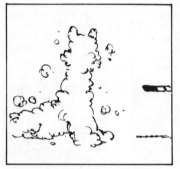

33..., 27..., 18...

HIKE!

AUGHH!

IT'S CLEAR I'LL NEVER HAVE A CAREER IN SPORTS UNTIL I LEARN TO SUPPRESS MY SURVIVAL INSTINCT.

TOUCH-DOWN!

WHAT THIS GAME NEEDS ARE NEGOTIATED SETTLEMENTS.

HOW COME *YOU'RE* THE ONE WHO GOES TO WORK, AND NOT MOM?

WELL, YOUR MOM *USED* TO GO TO WORK, BUT ONCE YOU CAME ALONG, SOMEONE HAD TO STAY HOME.

YOUR MOM'S JOB HAD A LOT OF STRESS AND AGGRAVATION, SEE,...

...AND SHE WANTED TO QUIT?

NO, SHE'D GOTTEN USED TO IT, SO WE FIGURED SHE SHOULD BE THE ONE TO...

HEY!

48

Get off the swing or I'll punch your lights out.

What a sissy! Haw!

YEARS FROM NOW, WHEN I'M SUCCESSFUL AND HAPPY, ...AND HE'S IN PRISON... I HOPE I'M NOT TOO MATURE TO GLOAT.

GIVE ME A NICE SMILE. THAT'S GOOD. NOW DON'T MAKE A FACE, OK? READY? ONE... TWO... THREE...

CLICK.

CLICK.

* CLICK *

OH, GREAT ALTAR OF PASSIVE ENTERTAINMENT...

BESTOW UPON ME THY DISCORDANT IMAGES AT SUCH SPEED AS TO RENDER LINEAR THOUGHT IMPOSSIBLE!

Calvin and Hobbes by WATTERSON

OUT IN THE FARTHEST REACHES OF THE GALAXY...

...SPEEDS THAT SPLENDID SPECIMEN OF SPIRIT AND SPUNK, THE SPECTACULAR *SPACEMAN SPIFF!*

THE FEARLESS SPACEMAN SPIFF SETS OFF TO EXPLORE A NEW PLANET!

THE PLANET APPEARS TO BE UNINHABITED. THE ONLY SIGN OF LIFE IS A STRANGE LICHEN GROWING ON THE ROCKS.

NOTICING THE GEOMETRIC PATTERNS THE LICHEN FORMS, SPIFF BENDS DOWN FOR A CLOSER LOOK.

IT'S NOT LICHEN! IT'S TINY TREES ON TINY FARMLAND!

PEERING AHEAD, OUR HERO SEES A SPRAWLING CITY, WITH SKYSCRAPERS AN INCH HIGH! THE PLANET IS INHABITED AFTER ALL!

SPIFF REFLECTS THAT HUMAN SCALE IS BY NO MEANS THE STANDARD FOR LIFE FORMS.

AS IF TO DRIVE THE POINT HOME, A BLIMP-SIZED MONSTER APPEARS OVER THE HILLSIDE!

Hey, lookit Shorty here! He's playing with his fellow bugs! Haw haw!

IT'S A *Doofus Ignoramus!* OUR HERO SLOWLY REACHES FOR HIS STUN BLASTER!

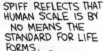

HERE IT IS 8:00 AND WE HAVE TO GO TO BED ALREADY.

SOMEBODY'S ALWAYS RUNNING MY LIFE. I NEVER GET TO DO WHAT *I* WANT TO DO.

WHAT WOULD YOU DO IF YOU COULD STAY UP?

I DUNNO... SOMETHING *FUN!* WHATEVER MOM AND DAD GET TO DO!

THAT CLOUD OF STARS IS OUR GALAXY, THE MILKY WAY. OUR SOLAR SYSTEM IS ON THE EDGE OF IT.

WE HURL THROUGH AN INCOMPREHENSIBLE DARKNESS. IN COSMIC TERMS, WE ARE SUBATOMIC PARTICLES IN A GRAIN OF SAND ON AN INFINITE BEACH.

I WONDER WHAT'S ON TV NOW.

EVERYONE TAKES ME FOR GRANTED! NOBODY PAYS ANY ATTENTION TO MY NEEDS!

IS IT TOO MUCH TO ASK FOR AN OCCASIONAL TOKEN GESTURE OF APPRECIATION?!

OK, HOW ABOUT A BIG HUG?

COULD I HAVE 20 DOLLARS?

SEE?! I DON'T MATTER TO ANYONE! NOBODY CARES ABOUT ME!

CALVIN and HOBBES by WATTERSON

Fig.1   *Fig.2*   *Fig.3*

HECK, I COULD MAKE A BETTER PICTURE THAN *THAT*.

C'MON, HOBBES, I'VE DECIDED TO BE A WILDLIFE PAINTER! WE'LL GO OUTSIDE AND YOU CAN POSE FOR ME.

OH BOY! I GET TO BE IN A PAINTING!

THIS LOOKS LIKE A GOOD NATURAL ENVIRONMENT. SIT ON THAT BIG ROCK.

VAN GOGH WOULD'VE SOLD MORE THAN ONE PAINTING IF HE'D PUT TIGERS IN THEM.

OK, YOU'RE LORD OF THE WILDERNESS! FROM YOUR PERCH YOU SURVEY YOUR TERRITORY WITH THE QUIET CONFIDENCE AND STEELY EYE OF A JUNGLE CAT!

LIKE THIS?

NO, THAT'S NOT QUITE IT.

THIS?

TOO FORMAL. LET'S TRY ONE WHERE THE FIERCE TIGER RESTS IN THE SHADE AFTER A KILL.

HOW'S THIS?

NO, NO.

NOW?

THIS ISN'T WORKING AT ALL.

HOW ABOUT THIS?

YES! THAT'S IT! HOLD THAT!

BOY, I HAD NO IDEA THIS WOULD BE SO HARD. CAN YOU IMAGINE POSING A DUMB *MOOSE*?

NOTICE I'M MORE OF A YELLOW OCHRE THAN A STRAIGHT ORANGE.

53

VROOM
VROOOM
RRR!

VROOM
VROOOOM

AUGHH!

I WOULDN'T MIND THIS SO MUCH IF HE DIDN'T KEEP A LOG.

WOULD YOU SAY YOU WERE "VERY SURPRISED" OR "COMPLETELY SURPRISED"?

LOOK MOM, I MADE A MASK.

ARE YOU GETTING READY FOR HALLOWEEN?

HUH? NO, THIS IS FOR EVERY DAY. YOU KNOW HOW HOBBES ALWAYS SNEAKS UP FROM BEHIND AND POUNCES ON ME?

NO...

WELL, HE DOES. BUT IF YOU WEAR A MASK LIKE THIS ON THE BACK OF YOUR HEAD, TIGERS CAN'T TELL WHICH WAY YOU'RE FACING, AND THEY CAN'T SNEAK UP.

I THINK YOUR TRAIN OF THOUGHT IS A RUNAWAY.

I READ THEY WEAR THESE IN INDIA. HERE, I MADE A MASK FOR YOU TOO.

HERE, DAD. I MADE YOU A MASK LIKE MINE. YOU WEAR IT ON THE BACK OF YOUR HEAD TO PREVENT TIGER ATTACKS.

UM...

TIGERS ALWAYS TRY TO GET YOU FROM BEHIND, BUT WITH THIS MASK ON, THEY CAN'T TELL WHICH WAY YOU'RE FACING, SO THEY DON'T POUNCE. I READ IT IN A BOOK.

WELL, I APPRECIATE YOUR CONCERN, BUT I THINK I'LL TAKE MY CHANCES AND NOT LOOK LIKE A LUNATIC.

OK, IF YOU'D RATHER LOOK LIKE RAW HAMBURGER, BE MY GUEST.

HONEY, ARE WE OUT OF ASPIRIN AGAIN?

WELL, IF IT ISN'T OL' ROCKET-BUTT! I GUESS YOU WON'T BE POUNCING ON *ME* ANY MORE! SEE, I'M WEARING A MASK ON THE BACK OF MY HEAD!

NOW YOU CAN'T TELL WHICH WAY I'M FACING, SO YOU CAN'T SNEAK UP FROM BEHIND! I'VE FINALLY THWARTED YOUR MURDEROUS RECREATION!

MAYBE THIS WILL TEACH YOU THAT *PEOPLE* ARE SMARTER THAN *ANIMALS!* YOU CAN'T OUTWIT A HUMAN!

NO FAIR! YOU DIDN'T EVEN SNEAK UP!

In the Middle Ages, lords and vassals lived in a futile system.

THAT'S "FEUDAL" SYSTEM.

JUST WHEN I THOUGHT THIS JUNK WAS BEGINNING TO MAKE SENSE.

I'M A GENIUS. I CAN'T BELIEVE HOW SMART I AM.

I'VE GOT MORE BRAINS THAN I KNOW WHAT TO DO WITH.

SO I'VE NOTICED.

WOO HOO HOO

Gimme that ball or I'll punch your face in.

Smart move, sissy boy.

IN MY OPINION, WE DON'T DEVOTE NEARLY ENOUGH SCIENTIFIC RESEARCH TO FINDING A CURE FOR JERKS.

OPEN WIDE... OPEN WIDE... ...THAT'S GOOD...

NOW THIS MIGHT CAUSE SOME SLIGHT DISCOMFORT... ...HOLD REAL STILL...

RRGGHH! MMF! RRG! STOP THRASHING! .. I'VE ALMOST GOT IT... ALMOST... MMF! **THERE!**

BOY, IT'S A GOOD THING YOU HAD THIS REMOVED! JUST LOOK AT ALL THESE BAD SPOTS!

LUNCH SHOULDN'T HAVE TO BE LIKE THIS.

TAKE A LOOK AT THIS. WOULDN'T YOU SAY THIS IS A GREAT DRAWING?

I MEAN, CAN YOU **BELIEVE** MY TEACHER DIDN'T LIKE IT? SHE SAID IT WASN'T "SERIOUS"!

BY GOLLY, IF THIS ISN'T SERIOUS ART, THEN NOTHING IS! WHO SET MISS WORMWOOD UP AS AN ARBITER OF AESTHETICS ANYWAY? THIS IS A BEAUTIFUL WORK OF POWER AND DEPTH!

IT'S A STEGOSAURUS IN A ROCKET SHIP, RIGHT?

SEE? **YOU** UNDERSTOOD IT!

Panel 1: ON THE ONE HAND, IT'S A GOOD SIGN FOR US ARTISTS THAT, IN THIS AGE OF VISUAL BOMBARDMENT FROM ALL MEDIA, A SIMPLE DRAWING CAN PROVOKE AND SHOCK VIEWERS. IT CONFIRMS THAT IMAGES STILL HAVE POWER.

Panel 2: ON THE OTHER HAND, MY TEACHER'S REACTIONARY GRADING SHOWS THAT OUR SOCIETY IS CULTURALLY IL-LITERATE AND THAT MANY PEOPLE CAN'T TELL GOOD ART FROM A HOLE IN THE GROUND.

Panel 3: THIS DRAWING I DID OBVIOUSLY CHALLENGES THE KNOW-NOTHING COMPLACENCY OF THOSE WHO PREFER SAFE, PREDIGESTED, BUCOLIC GENRE SCENES.

Panel 4: MY "C-" FIRMLY ESTABLISHES ME ON THE CUTTING EDGE OF THE AVANT-GARDE.

DON'T YOU HAVE TO WEAR SILLY CLOTHES THEN?

Panel 5: THE HARD PART FOR US AVANT-GARDE POST-MODERN ARTISTS IS DECIDING WHETHER OR NOT TO EMBRACE COMMERCIALISM.

Panel 6: DO WE ALLOW OUR WORK TO BE HYPED AND EXPLOITED BY A MARKET THAT'S SIMPLY HUNGRY FOR THE NEXT NEW THING? DO WE PARTICIPATE IN A SYSTEM THAT TURNS HIGH ART INTO LOW ART SO IT'S BETTER SUITED FOR MASS CONSUMPTION?

Panel 7: OF COURSE, WHEN AN ARTIST GOES COMMERCIAL, HE MAKES A MOCKERY OF HIS STATUS AS AN OUTSIDER AND FREE THINKER. HE BUYS INTO THE CRASS AND SHALLOW VALUES ART SHOULD TRANSCEND. HE TRADES THE INTEGRITY OF HIS ART FOR RICHES AND FAME.

Panel 8: OH, WHAT THE HECK. I'LL DO IT.

THAT WASN'T SO HARD.

Panel 9: TODAY I DREW ANOTHER PICTURE IN MY "DINOSAURS IN ROCKET SHIPS" SERIES, AND MISS WORMWOOD THREATENED TO GIVE ME A BAD MARK IN HER GRADE BOOK IF I DIDN'T STOP!

Panel 10: THE ARTS ARE UNDER ATTACK! FREEDOM OF EXPRESSION IS BEING SQUELCHED!

Panel 11: THE AUTHORITIES ARE TRYING TO SILENCE ANY VIEW CONTRARY TO THEIR OWN!

Panel 12: WHAT DOES YOUR TEACHER OBJECT TO ABOUT DINOSAURS?

MOSTLY MY DRAWING THEM DURING MATH.

ANOTHER GORGEOUS, BRISK FALL DAY.

WHAT A WASTE TO BE GOING TO SCHOOL ON A MORNING LIKE THIS.

WHAT WOULD YOU DO IF YOU COULD STAY HOME THIS MORNING?

SLEEP RIGHT THROUGH IT.

WHOA WHOAA WHOOOP

BONK AHHHH! OOF!

IT *COULD'VE* HAPPENED BY ACCIDENT!

DON'T SIT NEXT TO ME, CALVIN. I DON'T WANT TO HEAR ANY DISGUSTING COMMENTS ABOUT LUNCH.

RELAX. I WON'T TALK ABOUT LUNCH AT ALL.

INSTEAD, DO YOU WANT TO HEAR A RIDDLE I MADE UP?

A RIDDLE? OK.

WHAT'S THE DIFFERENCE BETWEEN A GARDEN SLUG AND A TWO-INCH-LONG, LIVING BOOGER?

EWW!!

I CAN'T THINK OF A DIFFERENCE EITHER.

CALVIN and HOBBES

by WATTERSON

THAT'S OUR SON! *SIGHHH*

THESE PICTURES WILL REMIND US OF MORE THAN WE WANT TO REMEMBER.

63

HELLO, IS YOUR DAD THERE?

NO, HE ISN'T.

OK, WILL YOU WRITE DOWN MY NUMBER AND HAVE HIM CALL ME?

HOLD ON. I NEED A PEN.

POW!

AGHH! I'VE BEEN SHOT!

I HATE TAKING MESSAGES.

MOM, DO WE HAVE A SHOE BOX I COULD HAVE? IT'S FOR A SCHOOL PROJECT.

I THINK SO. LET'S SEE.

HERE'S ONE. WHAT ARE YOU GOING TO DO WITH IT?

I'M SUPPOSED TO MAKE A DIORAMA. WE'RE STUDYING THE DIFFERENT ECO-SYSTEMS AND I'M GOING TO MAKE A DESERT SCENE.

THAT SOUNDS INTERESTING.

I'LL NEED SOME GLUE AND PAPER AND STUFF TOO. I'M GOING TO BUILD A CACTUS AND A ROADRUNNER.

WHEN IS THIS DUE?

IT WAS DUE TODAY, BUT I TOLD THE TEACHER I WASN'T QUITE FINISHED.

WOW, MOM SURE TURNED INTO THE CONNIPTION QUEEN WHEN SHE FOUND OUT I HADN'T EVEN STARTED MY DIORAMA PROJECT WHEN IT WAS ALREADY DUE TODAY.

SO THIS IS ONE DAY LATE! WHAT'S THE BIG DEAL?!

IT'S NOT AS IF *LIVES* HANG IN THE BALANCE, RIGHT? THE FATE OF THE UNIVERSE DOESN'T DEPEND ON TURNING IN A SHOE BOX DESERT SCENE ON TIME!

THAT'S KEEPING THINGS IN PERSPECTIVE.

EVEN IF LIVES *DID* HANG IN THE BALANCE, IT WOULD DEPEND ON WHOSE THEY WERE.

THIS IS HOPELESS! HOW AM I SUPPOSED TO CREATE A DESERT SCENE IN THIS SHOE BOX WHEN I DON'T EVEN KNOW WHAT A DESERT LOOKS LIKE?!

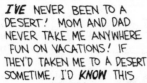

I'VE NEVER BEEN TO A DESERT! MOM AND DAD NEVER TAKE ME ANYWHERE FUN ON VACATIONS! IF THEY'D TAKEN ME TO A DESERT SOMETIME, I'D KNOW THIS STUFF!

WHY DON'T YOU GET OUT A BOOK?

AND GO TO ALL THAT TROUBLE?! YEAH, SURE! LOOK, I'M A BUSY GUY! I'VE GOT OTHER THINGS TO DO WITH MY LIFE BESIDES THIS, YOU KNOW!

RIGHT. WHY WASTE TIME LEARNING, WHEN IGNORANCE IS INSTANTANEOUS?

MY TV SHOW STARTS IN 20 MINUTES. ARE YOU GOING TO HELP ME OR NOT?

MOM, WHERE DO WE KEEP THE PAPIER-MÂCHÉ?

WE DON'T HAVE ANY.

OH GREAT! JUST GREAT! HOW AM I GOING TO MAKE A ROADRUNNER WITHOUT PAPIER-MÂCHÉ?!

MAYBE YOU SHOULD'VE THOUGHT OF THAT BEFORE 7:00 AT NIGHT. YOU'LL HAVE TO MAKE ONE SOME OTHER WAY.

BUT HOW?!

THIS IS YOUR SCHOOL PROJECT, CALVIN. YOU DO THE WORK.

IF I GET A BAD GRADE, IT'LL BE YOUR FAULT FOR NOT DOING THE WORK FOR ME!

HOW IS THE DIORAMA COMING ALONG?

I'M ALMOST FINISHED.

THAT DIDN'T TAKE TOO LONG.

THAT'S BECAUSE I'M A GENIUS.

I DON'T SEE THE ROADRUNNER. WEREN'T YOU GOING TO PUT ONE IN?

SEE THE COTTON BALLS I GLUED DOWN?

YEAH?

THE ROADRUNNER JUST RAN OUT OF THE SCENE, LEAVING THOSE CLOUDS OF DUST!

YOU'VE NEVER HAD AN OBLIGATION, AN ASSIGNMENT, OR A DEADLINE IN ALL YOUR LIFE! YOU HAVE NO RESPONSIBILITIES AT ALL! IT MUST BE NICE!

WIPE THAT INSOLENT SMIRK OFF YOUR FACE!

THE REAL FUN OF LIVING WISELY IS THAT YOU GET TO BE SMUG ABOUT IT.

I HATE DOING THIS STUFF! IT'S TOO MUCH WORK! WHY SHOULD I BOTHER?

"UNTIL YOU STALK AND OVERRUN, YOU CAN'T DEVOUR ANYONE."

I CAN SEE WHY TIGER APHORISMS DON'T CATCH ON.

"LIVE FOR THE MOMENT" IS MY MOTTO.

YOU NEVER KNOW HOW LONG YOU'VE GOT! YOU COULD STEP INTO THE ROAD TOMORROW AND - WHAM - YOU GET HIT BY A CEMENT TRUCK! THEN YOU'D BE SORRY YOU PUT OFF YOUR PLEASURES!

THAT'S WHY I SAY "LIVE FOR THE MOMENT." WHAT'S YOUR MOTTO?

"LOOK DOWN THE ROAD."

I'VE DECIDED I DON'T WANT TO BE FAMOUS.

NO?

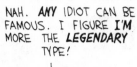

NAH. *ANY* IDIOT CAN BE FAMOUS. I FIGURE *I'M* MORE THE *LEGENDARY* TYPE!

UH HUH.

WELL I DIDN'T MEAN RIGHT THIS SECOND!

CAN WE BURN THESE LEAVES?

NO, THAT POLLUTES.

BUT HOW CAN WE APPEASE THE MIGHTY SNOW DEMONS IF WE DON'T SACRIFICE ANY LEAVES?! WE'LL HAVE A WARM WINTER!

I DON'T KNOW WHETHER YOUR GRASP OF THEOLOGY OR METEOROLOGY IS THE MORE APPALLING.

I GUESS I'LL GO LIGHT SOME CANDLES AROUND THE TOBOGGAN AND BEG FOR MERCY.

DO YOU THINK TIGERS GO TO THE SAME HEAVEN THAT PEOPLE GO TO?

I MEAN, IN HEAVEN, EVERYONE IS SUPPOSED TO BE *HAPPY*, RIGHT? BUT PEOPLE WOULDN'T BE HAPPY IF THEY WERE ALWAYS IN DANGER OF BEING EATEN BY TIGERS!

ON THE OTHER HAND, HEAVEN WOULDN'T BE VERY NICE *WITHOUT* TIGERS, EITHER. *I* WOULDN'T BE HAPPY IF THERE WEREN'T ANY TIGERS. I'D MISS THEM.

MAYBE TIGERS JUST DON'T EAT PEOPLE IN HEAVEN.

BUT THEN *HE* WOULDN'T BE HAPPY.

Calvin and Hobbes
by WATTERSON

WHY DO ANIMALS ALWAYS WALK IN CIRCLES BEFORE THEY LIE DOWN?

SORRY. PRIVILEGED INFORMATION.

Z

PSST! HEY KID!

MONSTERS!

WHAT DO YOU WANT?

THERE'S A BIG, SHINY TOY FOR YOU UNDER THE BED. COME GET IT!

OH SURE! YOU JUST WANT ME TO COME DOWN THERE SO YOU CAN GRAB ME WITH SOME OOZING APPENDAGE, SLOWLY PARALYZE ME WITH SOME VILE SECRETION, AND DEVOUR ME ALIVE! NICE TRY!   FORGET IT!

STUPID MONSTERS. ALL FANGS AND NO BRAINS.

PSST! TIGER! WE'LL GIVE YOU SOME SALMON IF YOU PUSH THE KID OVER THE BED!

IS THE SALMON FRESH?

HOLD ON, I'LL CHECK. ..YEAH, IT'S FRESH.

HOBBES, DON'T LISTEN TO THEM!!

HEY DAD, I'LL GUESS ANY NUMBER YOU'RE THINKING OF! GO AHEAD, PICK A NUMBER!

MM.... OK, I'VE GOT IT.

IS IT 92,376,051?

BY GOLLY, IT IS!

WAIT A MINUTE! YOU'RE JUST TRYING TO GET RID OF ME, AREN'T YOU?!

NO, YOU'RE PSYCHIC. GO SHOW MOM.

A LOT OF PEOPLE DON'T HAVE PRINCIPLES, BUT I DO! I'M A HIGHLY PRINCIPLED PERSON!

I LIVE ACCORDING TO ONE PRINCIPLE, AND I NEVER DEVIATE FROM IT.

WHAT'S YOUR PRINCIPLE?

"LOOK OUT FOR NUMBER ONE."

MOM, YOU KNOW THE SANDWICH YOU PACKED FOR ME TODAY? WELL, BY LUNCH TIME, THE JELLY HAD SOAKED INTO THE BREAD. THAT GROSSES ME OUT.

SO TOMORROW, I'D LIKE THE JELLY PUT IN A SEPARATE CONTAINER WITH A KNIFE, SO I CAN SPREAD THE JELLY AT THE LAST POSSIBLE MOMENT BEFORE I EAT THE SANDWICH.

ALSO, YOU KEEP USING BREAD FROM THE MIDDLE OF THE LOAF. I ONLY LIKE THOSE PIECES FOR TOAST. FOR SANDWICHES, I WANT ONLY THE END PIECES, BECAUSE THOSE DON'T ABSORB AS MUCH JELLY. GOT IT?

DOGGONE IT, SHE DID IT AGAIN!

WHY, LOOK! YOU MADE YOUR BED WITHOUT EVEN BEING TOLD TO! THAT'S WONDERFUL, CALVIN!

GEE, YOUR MOM SURE IS NICE WHEN YOU HELP HER.

YEAH. THAT'S THE REASON I USUALLY DON'T.

I LIKE MOM TO BE IMPRESSED WHEN I FULFILL THE LEAST OF MY OBLIGATIONS.

LOOK OUT THE WINDOW! IT'S SNOWING! THERE MUST BE ALMOST HALF AN INCH!

BY MORNING, I'LL BET THERE'S TONS OF SNOW! DO YOU THINK THE SCHOOLS WILL CLOSE??

WHAT? OH YEAH? WELL, SAME TO YOU!!

I WONDER HOW A CRABBY GUY LIKE HIM GOT TO BE SUPERINTENDENT.

THAT WAS QUITE A RIDE.

I'LL SAY.

I'VE NEVER SEEN A SLED CATCH FIRE BEFORE.

WE'RE LUCKY THE POND HADN'T FROZEN.

You just can't ever be too careful.

CHEATER.

HONEY, HAVE YOU SEEN MY GLASSES? I CAN'T FIND THEM ANYWHERE.

I HAVEN'T SEEN THEM.

CALVIN, GO DO SOMETHING YOU HATE! BEING MISERABLE BUILDS CHARACTER!

OK, THE VOICE WAS A LITTLE FUNNY, BUT THAT'S STILL ONE DARN SARCASTIC KID WE'RE RAISING.

AAGHH!!

THOSE CHILD PSYCHOLOGY BOOKS WE BOUGHT WERE SUCH A WASTE OF MONEY.

Calvin and Hobbes

THANK YOU, CLAIRE. THAT WAS VERY GOOD. .... ALL RIGHT, WHO'D LIKE TO GO NEXT?

ANYONE AT ALL, BESIDES CALVIN?

HEY!

FOR SHOW-AND-TELL, I BROUGHT THESE AMAZING FOSSILIZED BONE FRAGMENTS THAT I PAINSTAKINGLY UNEARTHED FROM SEDIMENTARY DEPOSITS IN MY FRONT YARD!

THOUGH THEY LOOK LIKE ORDINARY DRIVEWAY GRAVEL TO THE UNTUTORED EYE OF THE IGNORANT LAYMAN, I IMMEDIATELY RECOGNIZED THESE AS PIECES OF JAWBONE FROM A NEW SPECIES OF CARNOSAUR!

IN THIS DRAMATIC ILLUSTRATION, I'VE RE-CREATED THE COMPLETE *CALVINOSAURUS* AS IT WOULD HAVE APPEARED IN THE LATE JURASSIC! ITS COLORATION HERE IS SOMEWHAT CONJECTURAL.

I'LL BE PUBLISHING MY FULL FINDINGS SHORTLY! UNDOUBTEDLY, I'LL BE THE RECIPIENT OF MANY LUCRATIVE PALEONTOLOGY PRIZES, AND IN A MATTER OF WEEKS, PRESTIGE, FAME AND FORTUNE WILL BE MINE!

WHEN THIS HAPPENS, YOU CAN BE DARN SURE THAT THOSE OF YOU WHO WERE MEAN TO ME IN SCHOOL WILL SUFFER APPROPRIATELY!

I'LL EMPLOY MY RESOURCES TO MAKE YOUR PUNY LIVES MISERABLE! I'LL CRUSH YOUR PITIFUL DREAMS AND AMBITIONS LIKE BUGS IN THE DUST!

...BUT THERE *IS* AN ALTERNATIVE! I'M NOW ACCEPTING A LIMITED NUMBER OF APPLICATIONS TO BE MY PAL. THE COST IS JUST $20 PER PERSON, AND YOU CAN REVEL IN THE ASSOCIATION FOR A LIFETIME! ANY TAKERS?

OH YEAH? YOU JUST WAIT!

PRINCIPAL

Calvin and Hobbes

by WATTERSON

THERE.

NOW WE NEED TO GET THIS ON THE ROOF.

SANTA-- WEIGHED DOWN WITH EXTRA TOYS? DROP 'EM OFF HERE! --CALVIN

I'VE BEEN THINKING. THEY SAY SANTA KNOWS IF YOU'VE BEEN BAD OR GOOD, RIGHT?

RIGHT.

BUT THINK HOW MANY KIDS THERE ARE IN THE WHOLE WORLD! NOBODY COULD BE WATCHING EVERY KID EVERY SINGLE MINUTE! I MEAN, SANTA'S *OLD!* HE PROBABLY TAKES NAPS!

THE WAY *I* FIGURE IT, SANTA MUST JUST MAKE A FEW RANDOM CHECKS ON US ONCE OR TWICE A WEEK.

THAT'S ALL?

SURE. HE'D CATCH ENOUGH BAD KIDS THAT WAY TO SCARE EVERYONE ELSE INTO BEING GOOD MOST OF THE TIME. HE'D CREATE THE IMPRESSION HE'S WATCHING MORE THAN HE REALLY IS!

PRETTY SHREWD.

YEAH, BUT NOW THAT I'M ON TO HIM, I'M GOING TO GO SMACK SUSIE WITH A SNOWBALL! IF I DO IT QUICK, THE ODDS OF SANTA WATCHING ME AT THAT EXACT MOMENT ARE VIRTUALLY NIL!

WHAT IF SUSIE TELLS ON YOU?

OOH, I DIDN'T THINK OF THAT! SHE'S A GIRL, SO SHE PROBABLY *WOULD* SNITCH!

PHOOEY.

WELL I SURE HOPE SANTA'S WATCHING NOW, SEEING AS I'M BEING SO GOOD.

UNWILLINGLY GOOD, BUT GOOD NONETHELESS.

WATCHING A CHRISTMAS SPECIAL?

YEP.

ANOTHER SHOW EXTOLLING LOVE AND PEACE INTERRUPTED EVERY SEVEN MINUTES BY COMMERCIALS EXTOLLING GREED AND WASTE.

I HATE TO THINK WHAT YOU'RE LEARNING FROM THIS.

I'M LEARNING I NEED MY OWN TV SO I CAN WATCH SOMEPLACE ELSE.

I'M WRITING MY CHRISTMAS LIST, HOBBES! SHOULD I ADD ANYTHING FOR YOU?

HMM... I CAN'T THINK OF ANYTHING.

NOTHING?! YOU DON'T WANT ANYTHING AT ALL?!?

I'VE GOT A GOOD HOME AND A BEST FRIEND. WHAT MORE COULD A TIGER WANT?

IT MUST BE SAD BEING A SPECIES WITH SO LITTLE IMAGINATION.

THANKS FOR HELPING ME MAIL MY LETTER TO SANTA.

IT SURE WAS HEAVY.

THOSE BIG ENVELOPES ONLY HOLD A COUPLE HUNDRED PAGES. THAT'S WHY I USED A BOX.

I HOPE SANTA DOESN'T THROW HIS BACK OUT WHEN HE GETS IT.

ALL I CAN SAY IS, THIS YEAR SANTA HAD BETTER BRING EVERYTHING ON MY LIST! I'VE BEEN EXTREMELY GOOD ALL YEAR!

WHAT ABOUT THE NOODLE INCIDENT?

NO ONE CAN PROVE I DID THAT.!!

THIS WHOLE BUSINESS OF SANTA REWARDING *GOOD* KIDS AND NEGLECTING *BAD* KIDS REALLY BUGS ME.

...NOT THAT *I* HAVE ANYTHING TO WORRY ABOUT, OF COURSE.

A PARAGON OF VIRTUE, THAT'S YOU.

RIGHT! BUT SEE, THERE ARE CERTAIN THINGS A *GOOD* KID COULD DO THAT MIGHT LOOK *BAD* IN A CERTAIN LIGHT, IF ONE DIDN'T CONSIDER ALL THE MITIGATING CIRCUMSTANCES.

LIKE KEEPING AN INCONTINENT TOAD IN YOUR MOM'S SWEATER DRAWER?

EXACTLY. IF I WAS BEING RAISED IN A BETTER ENVIRONMENT, I WOULDN'T DO THINGS LIKE THAT.

I THINK IF SANTA IS GOING TO JUDGE MY BEHAVIOR OVER THE LAST YEAR, I OUGHT TO BE ENTITLED TO LEGAL REPRESENTATION.

I MEAN, LET'S FACE IT, A LOT OF CHRISTMAS LOOT IS AT STAKE HERE, AND THE CONSTITUTION SAYS NO PERSON SHALL BE DEPRIVED OF PROPERTY WITHOUT DUE PROCESS OF LAW.

SO YOU CAN BE MY LAWYER, OK? IT'S EASY!

ME??

SURE! HERE'S A LEGAL PAD! YOU'RE ALL SET!

OK, BUT I DON'T TAKE *PRO BONO* CASES.

OK, HOBBES, AS MY LAWYER, YOU'LL NEED TO REVIEW THE FACTS OF MY CASE.

RIGHT. WE'LL TRY TO ESTABLISH THAT YOU WERE INSANE AT THE TIME OF THE ALLEGED CRIMES.

WE'RE NOT COPPING AN *INSANITY* PLEA, YOU MORON! WE'RE SAYING I'M *INNOCENT!*

INSULTING AN ATTORNEY IS A PENAL OFFENSE, SO WATCH IT, BUSTER.

YOU'RE SUPPOSED TO ARGUE THAT I HAVEN'T BEEN BAD THIS YEAR, AND I DESERVE TO BE ON SANTA'S "GOOD" LIST!

IF *THAT'S* OUR CASE, I ADVISE YOU TO SETTLE OUT OF COURT.

IN A MINUTE, YOU AND *I* ARE GOING TO SETTLE THIS OUT OF *DOORS.*

SO LONG, MOM! HOBBES AND I ARE OFF TO THE NORTH POLE!

THE NORTH POLE?

YEP! WE'RE GOING TO SEE SANTA.

HOW COME? YOU ALREADY SENT HIM YOUR CHRISTMAS LIST.

YEAH, BUT I'M AFRAID SANTA MIGHT NOT HAVE CONSIDERED *MY* VERSION OF CERTAIN RECENT EVENTS. HOBBES IS GOING TO BE MY LAWYER AND PRESENT MY CASE.

JUST HOW RECENT ARE THESE RECENT EVENTS YOU'RE TALKING ABOUT?

GOTTA GO, MOM. IT'S A LONG WALK.

OK, HERE'S OUR STRATEGY: WHEN WE GET TO THE NORTH POLE, WE TELL SANTA THAT I'VE BEEN THE VICTIM OF MALICIOUS SLANDERS BY MY ENEMIES, AND WE'RE APPEALING TO HIM FOR JUSTICE.

WE SAY THAT I'M REALLY A *GOOD* KID... A GOOD KID WITH A GOOD HEART!

WE SAY I'M GOOD, GOOD, GOOD FROM THE MOMENT I GET UP UNTIL...

HEY! THERE'S SUSIE!

...UNTIL THE MOMENT A THOUGHT ENTERS YOUR HEAD.

I DON'T THINK SHE SAW US! QUICK, PACK SOME SLUSH-BALLS!

SUSIE'S STILL CONCENTRATING ON HER SNOWMAN! LET'S SNEAK UP AND BARRAGE HER WITH SLUSHBALLS!

TWO MINUTES AGO WE WERE ON OUR WAY TO TELL SANTA HOW *GOOD* YOU ARE, REMEMBER? HAVE YOU LOST YOUR MARBLES?!

OOPS. I FORGOT.

HOW MANY PRESENTS DO YOU THINK I'D FORFEIT FOR JUST ONE CLEAN SMACK UPSIDE SUSIE'S HEAD?

CALVIN and HOBBES

by WATTERSON

...and Santa, if I get any lords a-leaping or geese a-laying, you've **HAD** it.

HMM... THAT MIGHT NOT BE POLITIC.

I'M GETTING NERVOUS ABOUT CHRISTMAS.

YOU'RE WORRIED YOU HAVEN'T BEEN GOOD?

THAT'S JUST THE QUESTION. IT'S ALL RELATIVE. WHAT'S SANTA'S DEFINITION? HOW GOOD DO YOU HAVE TO BE TO QUALIFY AS GOOD?

I HAVEN'T **KILLED** ANYBODY. SEE, THAT'S GOOD, RIGHT? I HAVEN'T COMMITTED ANY FELONIES. I DIDN'T START ANY WARS. I DON'T PRACTICE CANNIBALISM.

WOULDN'T YOU SAY THAT'S PRETTY GOOD? WOULDN'T YOU SAY I SHOULD GET LOTS OF PRESENTS?

BUT MAYBE GOOD IS MORE THAN THE ABSENCE OF BAD.

SEE, *THAT'S* WHAT WORRIES ME.

...OK, ASSUMING I CAN GET AN OVERNIGHT LETTER TO THE NORTH POLE, WHAT WOULD YOU CHARGE TO WRITE ME A GLOWING CHARACTER REFERENCE?

OH NO, I'M NOT GOING TO PERJURE MYSELF FOR YOU! *MY* RECORD'S CLEAN!

WELL, THE SHOPPING IS DONE, THE PRESENTS ARE WRAPPED AND SENT, AND CALVIN'S IN BED. FOR THE FIRST TIME THIS MONTH, THERE'S NOTHING THAT HAS TO BE DONE.

I KNOW... SOMETIMES THIS SEASON REALLY SEEMS OUT OF CONTROL. WE DON'T OFTEN THINK ABOUT WHAT IT'S ALL SUPPOSED TO MEAN.

MM-HMM. IT'S GOOD TO SIT BY A COZY FIRE AND TAKE SOME QUIET TIME TO REFLECT.

WHAT'S *THIS*?! SANTA FLAMBÉ??

PSST! WAKE UP! MERRY CHRISTMAS, OL' BUDDY!

MERRY CHRISTMAS.

I DIDN'T GET YOU A PRESENT, BUT YOU'RE MY BEST FRIEND IN THE WORLD, HOBBES.

YOU'RE MY BEST FRIEND, TOO. I THINK THAT'S A GREAT GIFT.

WELL, ENOUGH OF THAT! IT'S ALMOST 4 AM! LET'S WAKE MOM AND DAD AND SEE WHAT SANTA BROUGHT US!

REMEMBER WE AGREED THAT IF SANTA GAVE YOU ANY SALMON, YOU'D SHARE IT!

DEAR GRANDMA,

THANK YOU FOR THE NICE BOX OF CRAYONS YOU SENT ME FOR CHRISTMAS.

THIS IS PROMPT.

OH YEAH, I ALWAYS SEND GRANDMA A THANK-YOU NOTE RIGHT AWAY.

...EVER SINCE SHE SENT ME THAT EMPTY BOX WITH THE SARCASTIC NOTE SAYING SHE WAS JUST CHECKING TO SEE IF THE POSTAL SERVICE WAS STILL WORKING.

THIS WILL BE THE STRONGEST SNOW FORT EVER BUILT!

UGHH

NGGHH

RGHH

MNHG

UNNHH

THERE! WE'RE SAFE FROM THAT SNOW GOON *NOW!*

I WONDER WHY WE HAVEN'T SEEN HIM FOR A WHILE.

HI CALVIN. NICE SNOW FORT.

I'LL SAY! THE WALLS ARE TWO FEET THICK AND WE'VE GOT 50 SNOWBALLS IN HERE!

WHO ARE YOU FIGHTING?

THERE'S A SNOW GOON RUNNING LOOSE! IF I WERE YOU, I WOULDN'T STICK AROUND. THIS COULD GET UGLY.

WHAT'S A SNOW GOON?

IT'S LIKE A SNOW MAN, BUT A GROTESQUE, EVIL, DEMENTED MONSTER.

OH, IS *THAT* WHAT ALL THOSE UGLY THINGS YOU MADE IN THE FRONT YARD ARE?

WHAT DO YOU MEAN, "ALL THOSE"?

LOOK! A *NEW* SNOW GOON!

THAT'S NOT THE ONE I MADE!

THE ORIGINAL SNOW GOON MUST BE MAKING HIS *OWN* SNOW GOONS!

OH NO!

I'LL BET HE'S MAKING AN ARMY! IN A FEW DAYS, HE COULD BUILD A HUNDRED SNOW GOONS! IF EACH OF *THEM* BUILT *ANOTHER* HUNDRED, AND THEN *THOSE* ALL BUILT A HUNDRED *MORE*, WHY...

...THAT WOULD BE PRETTY COOL, IF THEY WEREN'T OUT TO KILL ME.

I VOTE WE MAKE TRACKS FOR FLORIDA.

87

CALVIN, IT'S LATE! TIME TO COME IN!

I CAN'T, MOM! I'VE GOT TO KILL SNOW GOONS!

YOU CAN KILL THEM TOMORROW AFTER SCHOOL. C'MON INSIDE.

BUT BY TOMORROW, THERE WILL BE MORE OF THEM!

LET'S GO, CALVIN.

MOMS AND REASON ARE LIKE OIL AND WATER.

CAN YOU SEE THE SNOW GOONS OUT THERE?

YEAH. THEY'RE STILL MAKING MORE OF EACH OTHER.

HOW MANY DID YOU SEE?

ABOUT 15.

MAN, HOW AM I GOING TO GO TO SCHOOL TOMORROW? I'LL NEVER EVEN MAKE IT TO THE BUS STOP! I CAN'T OUTRUN 15 SNOW GOONS! I'M AS GOOD AS DEAD!

SWEET DREAMS.

YEAH, RIGHT! CAN I TAKE AN AX TO SCHOOL TOMORROW FOR ...UM... SHOW AND TELL?

THE SNOW GOONS AREN'T MOVING! THEY'RE ASLEEP!

NOW'S OUR CHANCE TO GO BUMP 'EM OFF!

WE CAN'T GO OUTSIDE NOW! IT'S 10 O'CLOCK AT NIGHT!

OH YEAH. MOM AND DAD ARE STILL UP.

WE'LL HAVE TO WAIT AT LEAST AN HOUR.

88

89

DAD, DON'T KILL ME! I CAN EXPLAIN THIS! HELP! HELP!

SNOW GOONS! I FROZE 'EM! THEY WERE GOING TO *GET* ME, SO I HAD TO GET THEM FIRST! ASK HOBBES!

CALVIN, IT IS AFTER MIDNIGHT. BELIEVE ME, WE WILL DISCUSS THIS *VERY* THOROUGHLY TOMORROW. YOU GET INTO BED THIS INSTANT.

LIKE I'M GOING TO GET ANY SLEEP *NOW*.

SEE?? SEE THE SNOW GOONS? I DIDN'T MAKE THEM! I MEAN, I MADE *ONE*, SORT OF BY ACCIDENT, BUT THE REST MADE THEMSELVES! THEY WERE BUILDING AN ARMY, SEE?

SEE, THAT'S WHY I HAD TO FREEZE THEM LAST NIGHT! I HAD TO GET 'EM WHILE THEY WERE SLEEPING! IT WAS MY ONLY CHANCE, SEE? SEE, IT ALL MAKES SENSE!

SEE? SEE??

THEY NEVER SEE.

WELL, HOBBES, I GUESS THERE'S A MORAL TO ALL THIS.

WHAT'S THAT?

"SNOW GOONS ARE BAD NEWS."

THAT LESSON CERTAINLY OUGHT TO BE INAPPLICABLE ELSEWHERE IN LIFE.

I LIKE MAXIMS THAT DON'T ENCOURAGE BEHAVIOR MODIFICATION.

CALVIN and HOBBES

by WATTERSON

A TINY SNOW-MAN!

WHY ARE YOU DOWN THERE WITHOUT A COAT?

ME? NO REASON.

I'M HO-OME!

!

YOU HAVE TO ADMIT IT'S SLOWED DOWN THE TRAFFIC ON OUR ROAD.

CALVIN!

ANY LUCK?

I'M SO DISAPPOINTED.

HEY JET PILOTS! DO A BARREL ROLL!

CALVIN and HOBBES

by WATTERSON

HEY HOBBES! ...HOBBES!

IT'S BEDTIME.

OOH, I WOULDN'T HAVE WANTED TO SLEEP THROUGH *THAT*.

I WONDER WHY WE DREAM WHEN WE SLEEP.

DO OUR BRAINS GET BORED? I WONDER WHY WE DON'T JUST PLAIN SLEEP.

I THINK WE DREAM SO WE DON'T HAVE TO BE APART SO LONG. IF WE'RE IN EACH OTHER'S DREAMS, WE CAN PLAY TOGETHER ALL NIGHT!

HEY, YEAH!

WELL, I'LL SEE YOU IN A FEW MINUTES, OL' BUDDY!

I'LL BE THERE!

Z   Z

CALVIN and HOBBES
by WATTERSON

His stabilizers useless, his fuel about to explode, our hero careens out of control over a strange, unexplored planet!

Yes, it's just another typical day for the incredible Spaceman Spiff!

Zorched by Zarches, Spaceman Spiff's crippled craft crashes on Planet Plootarg!

Dazed but undaunted, our fearless hero sets off in search of a service station!

Zounds! The zealous Zarches have followed Spiff to the planet's surface to finish him off!

With a sudden chill, our hero realizes the planet's soft, granular ground makes him easy to track!

Thinking quickly, Spiff runs backward, so his tracks show him going the OPPOSITE direction!

By continuing past a hiding place and doubling back, our hero fools the hideous aliens!

CALVIN! It's time to come in!

We know he went this way. We'll find him.

 TIME FOR BED, CALVIN.

 YOU CAN PUT MY BODY TO BED, BUT MY SPIRIT'S GOING TO STAY RIGHT HERE, SO WHY BOTHER? WHY SHOULDN'T I JUST STAY UP?

 BECAUSE THE BODY IS THE HOME OF THE SPIRIT, AND IF YOU'RE NOT IN BED IN TWO MINUTES, YOUR SPIRIT IS GOING TO BE PERMANENTLY NOMADIC.

 HOME SWEET HOME.

 THERE OUGHT TO BE A LAW AGAINST HAVING SCHOOL ON DAYS WHEN THERE'S ENOUGH SNOW TO PLAY IN.

 OF COURSE, I DON'T THINK THERE SHOULD BE SCHOOL IN THE **FALL** EITHER... AND SUMMER'S OUT ALREADY.... AND THEN THERE'S SPRING..

 I GUESS I'D GO TO SCHOOL A DAY IN NOVEMBER AND A DAY IN MARCH.

 BY SECOND GRADE, YOU'D BE PACKING YOUR LUNCH BOX WITH DENTURE CLEANERS.

AND BEFORE I GOT TO THIRD GRADE, I COULD RETIRE.

 HERE COMES THE GIANT SHIP! AHWOOOOOO! AHWOOOOOO!

 BUT WHAT'S THIS?! HE'S GOING FULL SPEED THROUGH THE DANGEROUS STRAIT!

 THE OIL TANKER CRASHED, MOM.

YOU POURED **INK** IN THE BATH WATER??

CALVIN and HOBBES
by WATTERSON

LET'S JUST SIT HERE A MOMENT...

..AND SAVOR THE IMPENDING TERROR.

HERE WE ARE, PERCHED AT THE PEAK OF MOUNT MAIM!

WHY? BECAUSE *I* LIKE TO EXPERIENCE LIFE TO THE FULLEST! *I* SAY YOU DON'T FULLY *APPRECIATE* LIFE UNTIL YOU RISK LOSING IT!

I LIKE TO STARE DEATH STRAIGHT IN THE EYE AND MAKE HIM BLINK! IF YOUR ADRENALIN ISN'T PUMPING, YOU'RE NOT REALLY LIVING!

RIGHT?

ACTUALLY, *I* THINK REAL LIVING IS SITTING BY A FIRE, SLURPING MARSH-MALLOWS FROM THE BOTTOM OF A MUG OF HOT COCOA.

SLURP

LOOK WHAT I MADE, HOBBES.

WHAT IS IT?

WHAT *IS* IT? WHY, IT'S A HUGE BIRD FOOT! I'M GOING TO PRESS IT IN THE SNOW AND MAKE EVERYONE THINK A TWO-TON CHICKADEE WALKED BY!

I GUESS TIME WEIGHS MORE HEAVILY ON SOME PEOPLE'S HANDS THAN OTHERS'.

HE'S JUST JEALOUS BECAUSE I ACCOMPLISH SO MUCH MORE THAN HE DOES.

HEY DAD, YOU KNOW HOW YOU WANTED ME TO SHOVEL THE DRIVEWAY? WELL I THOUGHT UP A *BETTER* IDEA!

I'LL SHOVEL AND PACK THE SNOW INTO A BIG RAMP! YOU CAN GET IN THE CAR, REV UP TO NEAR RED LINE, THROW OUT THE CLUTCH, LEAVE A PATCH OF MOLTEN RUBBER OUT THE GARAGE, AND ZOOM UP THE RAMP!

THEN WE COULD LINE BARRELS AND STUFF DOWN THE DRIVEWAY AND SEE HOW MANY YOU COULD CLEAR! WOULDN'T THAT BE GREAT??

I DON'T SEE WHY SOME PEOPLE EVEN *HAVE* CARS.

AUGHHH! A SNOW SNAKE'S GOT ME!

HORRIBLE INNER TEETH ON ITS SEPARATELY MOVING UPPER JAW BONES ARE PULLING ME DOWN ITS FRIGID GULLET! RUN FOR YOUR LIFE!

AT LEAST I *HAVE* A LIFE...UNLIKE SOME WEIRDOS I KNOW.

I SUPPOSE IF I HAD TWO X CHROMOSOMES, *I'D* FEEL HOSTILE TOO.

CALVIN and HOBBES

by WATTERSON

Calvin and Hobbes

by WATTERSON

WHILE LYING ON MY BACK TO MAKE
AN ANGEL IN THE SNOW,
I SAW A GREENISH CRAFT APPEAR!
A GIANT UFO!

A STRANGE, UNEARTHLY HUM IT MADE!
IT HOVERED OVERHEAD!
AND ALIENS WERE MOVING 'ROUND
IN VIEW PORTS GLOWING RED!

I TRIED TO RUN FOR COVER, BUT
A HOOK THAT THEY HAD LOW'R'D
SNAGGED ME BY MY OVERCOAT
AND HOISTED ME ABOARD!

EVEN THEN, I TRIED TO FIGHT,
AND THOUGH THEY NUMBERED MANY,
I POKED THEM IN THEIR COMPOUND EYES
AND PULLED ON THEIR ANTENNAE!

IT WAS NO USE! THEY DRAGGED ME TO
A PLATFORM, TIED ME UP,
AND WIRED TO MY CRANIUM
A FIENDISH SUCTION CUP!

THEY TURNED IT ON AND CURRENT COURSED
ACROSS MY CEREBELLUM,
COAXING FROM MY BRAIN TISSUE
THE THINGS I WOULDN'T TELL 'EM!

ALL THE MATH I EVER LEARNED,
THE NUMBERS AND EQUATIONS,
WERE MECHANIC'LY REMOVED IN THIS
BRAIN-DRAINING OPERATION!

MY ESCAPE WAS AN ADVENTURE.
(I WON'T TELL YOU WHAT I DID.)
SUFFICE TO SAY, I CANNOT ADD,
SO ASK SOME OTHER KID.

THERE'S SUSIE! HEH HEH! WATCH ME KNOCK HER FILLINGS LOOSE!

YAAA!

PIFF

YOU KNOW, I *THOUGHT* EARTH'S GRAVITY FELT EXCEPTIONALLY STRONG TODAY.

I GUESS THAT EXPLAINS HOW YOU SPILLED YOUR OATMEAL DOWN THE HEATER THIS MORNING.

OBVIOUSLY I CAN'T THROW SNOWBALLS AT SUSIE WHEN EARTH'S GRAVITY HAS INCREASED.

THIS IS A JOB FOR...

...FOR?

MOM MUST'VE PUT MY CAPE IN THE WRONG DRAWER!

SO WHO IS THIS A JOB FOR?

STUPENDOUS MAN!

MFF! GHH!

SUPER HEROES WEAR SNOW PANTS?

WHEN THERE'S SNOW OUT, THEY DO!

THIS LOOKS LIKE A *REAL* JOB FOR STUPENDOUS MAN!

WELL OF COURSE THE ZIPPER'S GOING TO GET STUCK IF EVERYONE STANDS AROUND *WATCHING* ME!

EARTH'S EXCESSIVE GRAVITY IS NO MATCH FOR *STUPENDOUS MAN'S* STUPENDOUS STRENGTH!

WITH MUSCLES OF MAGNITUDE, THE MASKED MAN OF MIGHT ROLLS A GIGANTIC SNOWBALL...

AND FLIES IT HIGH INTO THE *STRATOSPHERE*...

...WHERE HE USES HIS STUPENDOUS VISION TO LOCATE THE DIABOLICAL ARCH-FIEND *ANNOYING GIRL!*

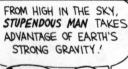

FROM HIGH IN THE SKY, *STUPENDOUS MAN* TAKES ADVANTAGE OF EARTH'S STRONG GRAVITY!

A DIRECT HIT! *STUPENDOUS MAN* TRIUMPHS!

WITH *ANNOYING GIRL* VANQUISHED, THE WHIRLWIND WONDER ZOOMS BACK TO RESUME HIS SECRET IDENTITY!

DID YOU SAVE THE DAY?

JUSTICE REIGNS ONCE MORE!

CALVIN, SUSIE'S MOM JUST CALLED. I WANT TO TALK TO YOU.

SUSIE'S MOM SAYS YOU DROPPED A SNOWBALL THE SIZE OF A BOWLING BALL ON SUSIE FROM A TREE.

IT COULDN'T HAVE BEEN *ME!* I'M VERY MILD-MANNERED.

SHE DESCRIBED EXACTLY THE HOOD AND CAPE I MADE YOU.

WHY, IT MUST'VE BEEN *STUPENDOUS MAN*, DEFENDER OF LIBERTY AND JUSTICE! I'M SURE SUSIE DESERVED WHATEVER SHE GOT.

LISTEN TO ME. YOU COULD HURT SOMEONE THAT WAY, AND IF I EVER HEAR OF ANYTHING LIKE THIS AGAIN, I'LL TAKE AWAY YOUR COSTUME FOR GOOD. GOT IT?

HMM, THIS SOUNDS LIKE *ANOTHER* JOB FOR STUPENDOUS MAN!

ACTUALLY, IT DOESN'T SOUND LIKE *QUITE* HIS TYPE OF JOB.

DAD, HOW DO SOLDIERS KILLING EACH OTHER SOLVE THE WORLD'S PROBLEMS?

I THINK GROWN-UPS JUST *ACT* LIKE THEY KNOW WHAT THEY'RE DOING.

HI HONEY! HOW WAS SCHOOL?

I GOT STUCK IN MY SNOW PANTS.

UH OH. WHAT HAPPENED?

WELL, THE ZIPPER GOT COVERED WITH ICE, SO I TRIED TO FORCE IT. THEN MY MITTEN GOT CAUGHT AND JAMMED THE ZIPPER.

I TRIED TO *PULL* MY SNOW PANTS OFF, BUT I FORGOT TO TAKE MY BOOTS OFF FIRST, SO *THOSE* GOT STUCK, AND THEN THE PANTS GOT ALL TWISTED, SO I FELL OVER, AND FINALLY THE TEACHER HAD TO CALL TWO CUSTODIANS TO GET ME OUT!

SO I WANT TO BE SURE TO WEAR THEM AGAIN TOMORROW.

LOOK, I'VE GOT SOME MODELLING CLAY!

WHAT ARE YOU MAKING?

THIS IS A HOOF.

A HOOF?

RIGHT! THIS WILL BE A LIFE-SIZE EQUESTRIAN STATUE OF ME!

A NEW HORSEMAN OF THE APOCALYPSE, HMM?

I THINK I'M GOING TO NEED MORE CLAY.

Calvin and Hobbes

by WATTERSON

I'VE DECIDED TO BE MORE OF A "PEOPLE" PERSON, AND MAKE MORE FRIENDS.

HOW COME?

I DON'T GET ENOUGH PRESENTS.

FROM NOW ON, I'M DEVOTING MYSELF TO THE CULTIVATION OF INTERPERSONAL RELATIONSHIPS.

AFTER ALL, NO MAN IS AN ISLAND. WE ALL NEED LOVE AND THE SUPPORT OF OTHERS. WE'RE SOCIAL BEINGS WITH SOCIAL NEEDS.

SO AS OF TODAY, MY GOAL IS TO BE AT ONE WITH MY FELLOW MAN, TO DEVELOP AND FOSTER THOSE DEEP CONNECTIONS THAT...... JUST A MINUTE....

HEY SUSIE! HEADS UP!! HA HA!! POW!

AUGH HELP HELP

I'VE CHANGED MY MIND, HOBBES. PEOPLE ARE SCUM.

I THINK *TRUE* HAPPINESS CAN ONLY BE FOUND IN THE WANTON INDULGENCE OF ANIMALS.

MY ESSAY IS ENTITLED, "AFTER SCHOOL AT MY HOUSE." ...AHEM...

"IT'S NOT THAT I *MIND* BEING CHAINED IN THE BASEMENT, IT'S JUST THAT WHEN THE MEAT IS THROWN DOWN, THE RATS HAVE THE ADVANTAGE OF NUMBERS, AND THEY..."

WHAT, MISS WORMWOOD?

ANOTHER PARENT-TEACHER CONFERENCE?!

I TOLD HER TO EXPECT YOU TO DENY EVERYTHING.

SSSS *SNAP* FSSSST

POP!

SNARRLL

YOMP GRRRR

FSSSSS PSSSTSS

GRRRR

THAT'S WHY *I'M* WAY OVER *HERE.*

MOMM! MOM!

WHAT'S THE MATTER?? WHAT'S WRONG?!

HOBBES WANTS A SECOND GOOD NIGHT KISS.

IT'S TWO IN THE MORNING!!

HE SAYS THE FIRST KISS DIDN'T TAKE.

HMPH. I DON'T THINK *THAT* ONE TOOK EITHER.

OH GO TO SLEEP.

CALVIN and HOBBES

by WATTERSON

THE DISTANT PLANET Z-12.

DISTANT, THAT IS, TO EVERYONE BUT *SPACEMAN SPIFF!*

THE FEARLESS EXPLORER SPACEMAN SPIFF CRUISES OVER THE DESOLATE DUNES OF AN UNCHARTED PLANET!

NO VEGETATION COVERS THE ROLLING TERRAIN. MILLIONS OF YEARS OF HARSH EXPOSURE WITHOUT AN ATMOSPHERE HAS SWEPT THE SURFACE CLEAN.

WHAT STRANGE CHEMICALS MUST COMPOSE THIS ALIEN SOIL! CROSSING A RIFT, THE ROCKS ABRUPTLY CHANGE COLOR!

ZOUNDS! A HUGE MOUNTAIN SUDDENLY RISES OUT OF THE PLAIN! OUR HERO PULLS UP!

OVER THE TOP, SPIFF DISCOVERS IT'S NOT A MOUNTAIN AT ALL! THE WHOLE LANDSCAPE IS... IS *BEDDING* FOR A HORRENDOUS MONSTER!

ZG! MF! WHUH? ALL RIGHT, WHAT TIME IS IT?!

THE CREATURE APPEARS HOSTILE! WITH NO TIME TO LOSE, OUR HERO READIES A HYDRO BOMB!

AUGH!
WHO DID THIS?!

THE DAME'S SCREAM HIT AN OCTAVE USUALLY RESERVED FOR CALLING DOGS, BUT IT MEANT I HAD A CASE, AND THE SOUND OF GREENBACKS SLAPPING ACROSS MY PALM IS MUSIC TO *MY* EARS ANY DAY. AFTER ALL, I'M NOT AN OPERA CRITIC. I'M A PRIVATE EYE.

I KEEP TWO MAGNUMS IN MY DESK. ONE'S A GUN, AND I KEEP IT LOADED. THE OTHER'S A BOTTLE AND IT KEEPS *ME* LOADED. I'M TRACER BULLET. I'M A PROFESSIONAL SNOOP.

IT'S A TOUGH JOB, BUT THEN, I'M A TOUGH GUY. SOME PEOPLE DON'T LIKE AN AUDIENCE WHEN THEY WORK. ENOUGH OF THEM HAVE TOLD ME SO WITH BLUNT INSTRUMENTS THAT I'M A PHRENOLOGIST'S DREAM COME TRUE.

SNOOPING PAYS THE BILLS, THOUGH. ESPECIALLY BILL, MY BOOKIE, AND BILL, MY PROBATION OFFICER.

SO WHEN A TALL BRUNETTE OPENED MY DOOR WITH A CASE FOR ME, MY HEART DID A FEW CALISTHENICS AND I TOOK THE JOB.

THE DAME SAID SHE HAD A CASE. SHE SOUNDED LIKE A CASE HERSELF, BUT I CAN'T CHOOSE MY CLIENTS.

SHE WAS THE PUSHY TYPE. THE KIND WHO'D BREAK YOUR HEART, OR MAYBE YOUR ARMS. I HURRIED OVER.

EITHER SHE HAD A PSYCHOTIC DECORATOR, OR HER PLACE HAD BEEN RANSACKED BY SOMEONE IN A BIG HURRY.

WELL?! HOW DO YOU EXPLAIN THIS?

THE DAME WAS HYSTERICAL. DAMES USUALLY ARE.

WHAT HAVE YOU GOT TO SAY FOR YOURSELF?

DON'T TOUCH ANYTHING. I'M LOOKING FOR CLUES.

THE CLICK OF A HAMMER BEING COCKED BEHIND MY HEAD FOCUSED MY THOUGHTS LIKE ONLY A LOADED .38 CAN.

THE DAME HAD SET ME UP! SHE DIDN'T WANT ME TO SOLVE THE CASE AT ALL! SHE JUST WANTED A PATSY TO PIN THE CRIME ON!

WELL?

I DIDN'T LIKE THE WAY THIS STORY WAS SHAPING UP, SO I DECIDED TO WRITE A NEW ENDING WITH MY .45 AUTOMATIC AS CO-AUTHOR.

I INTRODUCED THE DAME TO A FRIEND WHO'S VERY CLOSE TO MY HEART. JUST A LITTLE DOWN AND LEFT, TO BE SPECIFIC.

MY FRIEND IS AN ELOQUENT SPEAKER. HE MADE THREE PROFOUND ARGUMENTS WHILE I EXCUSED MYSELF FROM THE ROOM. I ALWAYS LEAVE WHEN THE TALK GETS PHILOSOPHICAL.

YOU'RE IN *REAL* TROUBLE NOW, YOUNG MAN!!

I'D JUST FINISHED PUTTING THE PUZZLE PIECES TOGETHER WHEN THE DAME'S HIRED GOON JUMPED OUT OF NOWHERE AND PRACTICED FOR HIS CHIROPRACTIC DEGREE.

WHEN HE WAS DONE, AN ALL-PERCUSSION SYMPHONY WAS PLAYING IN MY HEAD, AND THE ACOUSTICS WERE INCREDIBLE. THE ORCHESTRA WENT ON A TEN-CITY TOUR OF MY BRAIN, AND I HAD A SEASON PASS WITH FRONT ROW SEATS.

I HAD FIGURED OUT WHO TRASHED THE DAME'S LIVING ROOM, BUT SINCE SHE WASN'T MY CLIENT ANY MORE, I FELT NO NEED TO DIVULGE THE INFORMATION.

BESIDES, THE CULPRIT HAPPENED TO BE A BUDDY OF MINE. I CLOSED THE CASE.

I GUESS WE SHOULD'VE PLAYED OUTSIDE, HUH?

WHAT'S UP TODAY?

NOTHING SO FAR.

"SO FAR"?

WELL, YOU NEVER KNOW. SOMETHING *COULD* HAPPEN TODAY.

AND IF ANYTHING *DOES*, BY GOLLY, I'M GOING TO BE READY FOR IT!'

I NEED A SUIT LIKE THAT.

I JUST SAW A COMMERCIAL FOR A LUXURY CRUISE. HOW COME *WE* DON'T EVER GO ON VACATIONS LIKE THAT?

VACATIONS ARE ALL JUST A MATTER OF COMPARISON.

HUH?

WE SPEND A WEEK IN COLD, UNCOMFORTABLE TENTS EACH YEAR SO LIVING *HERE* THE REST OF THE TIME SEEMS LIKE A LUXURY CRUISE. IF YOUR TRIPS ARE UNPLEASANT, YOUR WHOLE *LIFE* IS A VACATION!

PLEASE TELL ME I'M ADOPTED.

YOU KNOW, I DON'T THINK MATH IS A SCIENCE. I THINK IT'S A RELIGION.

A RELIGION?

YEAH. ALL THESE EQUATIONS ARE LIKE MIRACLES. YOU TAKE TWO NUMBERS AND WHEN YOU ADD THEM, THEY MAGICALLY BECOME ONE *NEW* NUMBER! NO ONE CAN SAY HOW IT HAPPENS. YOU EITHER BELIEVE IT OR YOU DON'T.

THIS WHOLE BOOK IS FULL OF THINGS THAT HAVE TO BE ACCEPTED ON FAITH! IT'S A RELIGION!

AND IN THE PUBLIC SCHOOLS NO LESS. CALL A LAWYER.

AS A MATH ATHEIST, I SHOULD BE EXCUSED FROM THIS.

AUGHH

CALVIN AND HOBBES

by WATTERSON

BOK BOK BOK
BOK

I KIND OF RESENT THE MANUFACTURER'S IMPLICIT ASSUMPTION THAT THIS WOULD AMUSE ME.

HEY DAD, HOBBES SAYS THAT TIGERS ARE MORE PERFECTLY EVOLVED THAN HUMANS!

HE SAYS THAT IF THE PLAYING FIELD WAS LEVEL AND WE DIDN'T HAVE GUNS, PEOPLE WOULD BE NOTHING BUT **CAT FOOD!** TELL HIM THAT'S NOT...

THERE! 10 CENTS.

WE BET A QUARTER, YOU CHISELER.

BU-URRPP!

CLAP CLAP CLAP CLAP CLAP CLAP

AUTHOR! AUTHOR!

ENCORE!

PHILISTINES.

I'M NOT GOING TO SCHOOL TODAY.

OH, YOU'RE NOT?

NOPE! I'M STAYING HOME AND WATCHING TELEVISION ALL DAY!

APPARENTLY I WAS MISINFORMED.

TODAY FOR SHOW AND TELL I BROUGHT ONE OF MY OWN PATENT PENDING INVENTIONS!

I HAVE IN MY HAND AN INVISIBLE CRETINIZER! ONE SHOT RENDERS THE VICTIM A BABBLING SIMP, A DOLT, AN UTTER MORON!

OH SURE, CALVIN! GIVE US A BREAK!

AS RONALD PROVES, IT'S QUITE EFFECTIVE, EVEN AT LONG RANGE.

HEY!

FIND ANY DINOSAUR BONES YET?

NOPE.

I WISH WE LIVED IN THE BADLANDS OF MONTANA. IT'S EASIER THERE BECAUSE EROSION OFTEN EXPOSES THE BONES.

HERE THOUGH, YOU JUST HAVE TO START DIGGING AND HOPE FOR THE BEST.

HENCE THE SYSTEMATIC APPROACH; HMM?

RIGHT, I GUESS I'LL HAVE TO MOVE THAT SAPLING.

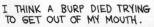

CALVIN and HOBBES

by WATTERSON

NYUP NCHYUP

I THINK A BURP DIED TRYING TO GET OUT OF MY MOUTH.

I'M THIRSTY.

THUMP

MONSTER EYES!

HELP HELP! IT'S AFTER ME!

IT'S *GOT* ME! I CAN FEEL ITS TERRIBLE FANGS.!! CRASH BONK

SLEEPWALKING AGAIN!

LET'S GO BACK TO BED, HONEY. YOU HAD A NIGHTMARE.

OH, IT WAS *YOU*!

IT SURE IS CREEPY HAVING A FRIEND WHOSE EYES GLOW IN THE DARK.

IT'S SO WE CAN SEE PEOPLE WHO MIGHT BE SNEAKING OUT OF BED TO FIX A SNACK WITHOUT MAKING ARRANGEMENTS TO SHARE.

WELL LOOK AT YOU! DON'T YOU LOOK NICE AND NEAT!

YES, I BELIEVE IN THE IMPORTANCE OF GOOD GROOMING.

SPEAKING OF WHICH, I'D BETTER GET IN THE TUB IF I WANT TO BE IN BED ON TIME.

JUST WHAT ARE YOU UP TO?

I HEARD CALVIN SPLASHING IN THE TUB, BUT THERE'S NO WATER ON THE FLOOR.

HIS TOWEL IS HUNG TO DRY! THE TOOTHPASTE CAP IS ON! THERE'S NO MESS ANYWHERE!

AND YOU'RE ALREADY IN BED??

WOULD YOU CHECK OVER MY HOMEWORK TONIGHT, SO I CAN CORRECT ANY MISTAKES IN THE MORNING BEFORE SCHOOL? THANKS, MOM.

GOOD MORNING, MOM.

YOU'RE UP AND DRESSED?! I DIDN'T EVEN CALL YOU!

I LIKE TO GET UP EARLY SO THE MORNING ISN'T RUSHED.

AND WITH THE EXTRA TIME, I CAN REVIEW MY ASSIGNMENTS AND BE BETTER PREPARED FOR CLASS.

I'M BRACING MYSELF FOR WHEN THE OTHER SHOE DROPS.

DON'T GET UP. I'LL FIX MY OWN BREAKFAST. DO WE HAVE ANY PRUNES?

I MADE MY BED AND I PUT MY BREAKFAST DISHES AWAY! I'M OFF TO SCHOOL NOW!

HAVE A GOOD DAY.

THANK YOU. I'LL STUDY HARD. A GOOD EDUCATION IS INVALUABLE.

THIS IS WORKING OUT GREAT!

I CAN'T BELIEVE YOUR MOM THINKS THAT'S YOU.

I'VE GOT TO SAY, HOBBES, I'VE REALLY PERFECTED MY OLD DUPLICATOR THIS TIME!

I'LL GRANT IT NEEDED PERFECTING.

IT WAS SO SIMPLE TO ADD AN ETHICATOR! I DON'T KNOW WHY I DIDN'T THINK OF IT BEFORE!

NOW, INSTEAD OF MAKING A COMPLETE DUPLICATE OF ME, I'VE MADE A DUPLICATE OF JUST MY GOOD SIDE! HE DOES ALL THE WORK AND I GET ALL THE CREDIT! HE'S A TOTAL SAP!

I KNOW! I KNOW THE ANSWER!

YOU'VE GOTTEN SO MANY, LET'S LET SOMEONE ELSE TRY THIS ONE, OK, DEAR?

LAST TIME YOU MADE A DUPLICATE OF YOURSELF, THE DUPLICATE MADE DUPLICATES, REMEMBER? IT WAS A MESS!

TRUE, BUT THANKS TO THE ETHICATOR, IT CAN'T HAPPEN THIS TIME!

BY ONLY DUPLICATING MY GOOD SIDE, I'VE ENSURED THAT THIS DUPLICATE WON'T CAUSE ANY TROUBLE! HE'S A COMPLETE BOY SCOUT!

THERE'S NOTHING THIS TWERP LIKES BETTER THAN MAKING EVERYONE'S LIFE EASIER! HE LIVES FOR IT!

THE ETHICATOR MUST'VE DONE SOME DEEP DIGGING TO UNEARTH HIM!

TALK ABOUT SOMEONE EASY TO EXPLOIT!

WHEN YOU'RE DONE PUTTING MY TOYS AWAY, YOU CAN GET TO WORK ON MY MATH ASSIGNMENT.

OK.

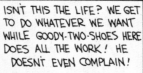

ISN'T THIS THE LIFE? WE GET TO DO WHATEVER WE WANT WHILE GOODY-TWO-SHOES HERE DOES ALL THE WORK! HE DOESN'T EVEN COMPLAIN!

VIRTUE IS ITS OWN REWARD.

HE DOESN'T COMPLAIN, BUT HIS SELF-RIGHTEOUSNESS SURE GETS ON MY NERVES.

HELLO, MAY I CARRY YOUR BOOKS FOR YOU?

WHY? SO YOU CAN THROW THEM IN A PUDDLE OR SOMETHING? FORGET IT!

I WOULDN'T DO THAT!

YEAH, YOU'D PROBABLY DO SOMETHING **WORSE**! YOU'RE NOT TOUCHING MY BOOKS, CALVIN!

STRICTLY SPEAKING, I'M NOT CALVIN. I'M THE PHYSICAL MANIFESTATION OF CALVIN'S **GOOD** SIDE.

IF THAT WAS TRUE, YOU'D BE A LOT SMALLER.

BOY, HAVE I HEARD **THAT** JOKE A LOT.

AND IF YOU THINK YOU CAN GET MY BOOKS BY ACTING EVEN WEIRDER THAN USUAL, THINK AGAIN!

SAY, CALVIN, THAT NICE GIRL DOWN THE STREET SEEMS TO THINK YOU'RE A TOTAL JERK.

WHO, SUSIE? YOU WEREN'T TALKING TO SUSIE, WERE YOU?

YES. I OFFERED TO CARRY HER BOOKS AND SHE...

YOU DID **WHAT**?!

SHE CLEARLY DOESN'T TRUST YOU AT ALL.

OH, MAN! NOBODY **SAW** YOU, DID THEY?! THEY'LL THINK IT WAS **ME**! YOU WANT TO MAKE IT LOOK LIKE I **LIKE** HER?!

SHE SEEMED UPSET, SO THIS AFTERNOON I TOOK HER SOME FLOWERS I PICKED, BUT...

AUGHH! AUGHH! AUGHH!

121

CalviN aNd HobbEs

by WATTERSON

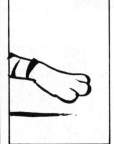

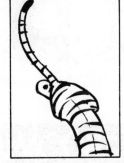

I THINK THESE COMIC BOOKS HE READS ARE MUCH TOO GRIM.

MUST BE! JUST LOOK AT HIM TWITCH.

WELL, THAT'S THE END OF CHAPTER ONE. WE'LL STOP HERE.

NO, READ THE WHOLE BOOK, OK?

CALVIN, THERE'S A HUNDRED MORE PAGES AND IT'S LATE. WE'LL READ ANOTHER CHAPTER TOMORROW.

NO, NO! FINISH IT TONIGHT!

GEE, YOU MUST REALLY LIKE THIS.

I HAVE TO WRITE A PAPER ON IT TOMORROW.

YOU KNOW WHAT I'VE NOTICED, HOBBES? THINGS DON'T BUG YOU IF YOU DON'T THINK ABOUT THEM.

SO FROM NOW ON, I SIMPLY WON'T THINK ABOUT ANYTHING I DON'T LIKE, AND I'LL BE HAPPY ALL THE TIME!

DON'T YOU THINK THAT'S A PRETTY SILLY AND IRRESPONSIBLE WAY TO LIVE?

WHAT A PRETTY AFTERNOON.

WHAT ARE YOU DOING OUT IN THE RAIN?

I'M ENGAGED IN A CONTEST OF WILLS! IT'S ME AGAINST NATURE!

WHICH OF US IS GOING TO GIVE UP FIRST? IS NATURE GOING TO GIVE UP AND STOP RAINING, OR AM I GOING TO GIVE UP AND GO INSIDE? SO FAR, IT'S UNDECIDED, BUT I'M DETERMINED TO WIN!

KABOOM!

OOOH, BIG NOISE! YOU DON'T SCARE ME! KEEP IT COMING! I'M NOT GOING IN!

POOR GUY JUST COULDN'T STAND THE SUSPENSE.

CALVIN and HOBBES
by WATTERSON

UH OH, HERE COMES CALVIN...

..THE INCURABLE WEIRDNESS POSTER CHILD.

HI CALVIN. WHAT'S WITH THE MASK AND BUCKET?

HMPH.

THIS IS A POEM! PLEASE DO WHAT YOU'RE TOLD! AND HERE IS A BUCKET, OF WATER, ICE-COLD!

PLEASE TAKE THIS WATER, AND DUMP IT ON ME! DON'T HESITATE! DO IT A.S.A.P.!

JUST WAIT TILL *YOU* TOUCH THE "PERNICIOUS POEM PLACE"!! OOOH, YOU'LL BE SORRY *THEN*!

WHEEE! I LOVE PLAYING CALVINBALL! THIS IS A BAG FLAG ZONE!

MR. SUBTLETY DRIVES HOME ANOTHER POINT.

126

The End